HORARY ASTROLOGY

The art of astrological divination.

D1131884

HORARY ASTROLOGY

by

Derek Appleby

THE AQUARIAN PRESS
Wellingborough, Northamptonshire

First published 1985

British Library Cataloguing in Publication Data

Appleby, Derek
  Horary astrology.
  1. Horoscopes
  I. Title
  133.5'4   BF1728.A2

ISBN 0-85030-380-X

The Aquarian Press is part of the Thorsons Publishing Group

Printed and bound in Great Britain

CONTENTS

ACKNOWLEDGEMENTS

My special thanks and appreciation to Bridget for valuable assistance and support; to Michael Hudson for listening patiently; to Geoffrey Cornelius for constructive criticism; to Maggie Hyde, Gordon Watson, Jane Farrer, Vern Wells, Olivia Barclay, Sheila MacLeod, Pat Harding, Carole Barnes, Katherine Howard, Maurice McCann, and all my astrological friends, for their co-operation and constant encouragement.

To Councillor Kate and Sally

PART ONE:
THE METHODS
OF HORARY ASTROLOGY

1.
CHARTING THE QUESTION

Quite simply, horary astrology is the art of astrological divination. A question is posed; the astrologer erects a chart for the moment of the question, and then makes a judgement as to the likely outcome of the matter enquired about. Each horary case is a unique challenge. When a question is put in good faith, and the chart conforms to certain conditions so that it is able to be judged, the answer to the question is locked up in the chart somewhere. The astrologer must employ all his skill, all his intuition and imagination, in breaking the code of the heavens and making a judgement. Sometimes the answer is a clear yes or no, but often the matter requires much consideration and concentration before the astrologer feels able to pronounce, if at all; for the heavens hide their secrets with extreme cunning.

Time and Location
When a question is received by the astrologer, his first task is to draw a chart for the moment the question was posed. The method used for setting up a horary chart for the birth of a question is the same as for any other birth moment, apart from a few adjustments concerning time and location.

Figure 1 is the chart for a question I asked myself. (One may act as one's own astrologer.) At the time, I was working for a large brewery and was not happy. A friend had recently begun working for another brewery and she seemed very happy. I asked her to tell me if she heard of a vacancy within her company that might suit me. Shortly afterwards she telephoned to say that an internal advertisement had been issued for the sort of job I was looking for. I was most interested, but I did not feel able to reply to an internal advertisement. However, I decided to ask the question: Will I get the job? I promised myself that if the chart was favourable I would write to the company expressing interest.

This example immediately demonstrates the unique value of horary astrology. It allows the astrologer to isolate a particular situation and make a judgement about a certain course of action. One is able to 'zoom in' on a specific issue.

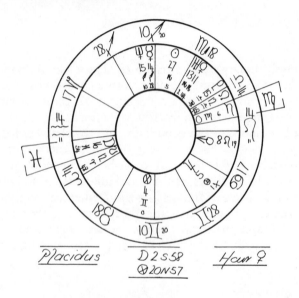

Figure 1.   Will I get the job? 19 November 1977, 12PM43 GMT
51N46 OW28.

Figure 1 is timed for the moment the question formed itself in my mind. If someone else had asked the question, the chart would have been drawn for the moment the question was posed and located for the place of our meeting. If the question had been asked over the telephone, the chart would have been timed for the moment the question was asked and located for the place the questioner was speaking from. For a question contained within a letter, the chart should be timed for the moment the astrologer reads the question and located for the place the letter is written from. In all other respects the calculation of a horary chart is the same as for a nativity.

House Division

The charts demonstrated in this book have either *Placidus* or *Regiomontanus* cusps. The issue of house division is a matter for the individual astrologer, you must settle with whatever system you find most comfortable. My own experience tells me that *equal house* division is unsuitable for horary work, though not necessarily for other matters. Al Morrison of New York, a respected astrologer, varies his system of house division according to the nature of the question, and he is well worth hearing on the subject. William Lilly (1602-1681), a grand master of horary astrology, always used Regiomontanus; and Lilly is the main reference source for most horary works. I would suggest that Placidus is used to begin with, if only because the tables are readily available. Later you might wish to experiment with alternative systems. The reason for the mix in this book is that I began with Placidus but have now settled with Regiomontanus.

The Nodes and Parts

When drawing the chart always include the North and South Nodes, and the Part of Fortune (Fortuna). If a question in any way concerns death, include the Part of Death, or sickness — the Part of Sickness; for a query related to marriage, insert the Part of Marriage.

The Part of Fortune is derived from: the Ascendant plus the Moon minus the Sun.

It is written thus: ⊗

The Part of Death is derived from: the Ascendant plus the eighth cusp minus the Moon.

It is written thus: Ⓓ

The Part of Sickness is derived from: the Ascendant plus Mars minus Saturn.

It is written thus: Ⓢ

The Part of Marriage is derived from: the Ascendant plus the Descendant minus Venus.

It is written thus: Ⓜ

These parts are just a few of many. They are generally known as Arabian Parts but there is evidence that the Arabs acquired the basic idea from the Greeks and developed it. The four given above are very commonly used in horary astrology, but there is room for a great deal of experiment in the use of Arabian Parts.

The Nodes, North (Dragon's Head) ☊ and South (Dragon's Tail) ☋, may be found in any ephemeris. The former is regarded as benefic and of the nature of Jupiter, and the latter malefic and of the nature of Saturn. Not enough is known about their influence to make firm statements about their effects, but it is safe to assume that the North is benefic and the South malefic.

One of the most common points of confusion among students concerns the moment for which a chart should be drawn when a question has been lingering in the mind for some time and the moment it first came into consciousness cannot be isolated or recalled. In such cases the *potent moment* is when one mentally decides to erect a chart for the question; or, if the question is posed by another, the moment it is asked of you — the astrologer.

Before you even begin to draw a chart, make a definite decision as to whether or not to accept the question. Avoid giving judgement upon frivolous matters, and do not accept questions merely designed to test your art. The question should be put in good faith with a genuine desire for serious judgement.

The Judgement of Events and Contests

It is true to say that other potent moments, aside from specific questions, may be examined for their potential in a similar way to that employed in horary judgements. Such events as interviews, medical consultations, appointments, disasters, contests and competitions may be enquired about through astrology. However, there are important differences in approach, and I have no intention of mixing the judgement of horary questions with the judgement of events in this book. In my opinion the judgement of events, etc., is a separate area of astrological investigation.

Preparation — Stage One

1. Consider the question and decide whether to accept or reject it; reject frivolous questions; accept questions put in good faith.

2. Time and locate the chart as follows: *For your own question* — the time and place the question first occurred to you.
   Questions put directly by another — the time the question was asked and the place of the meeting.
   Questions asked by telephone — the time the question was put and the place the questioner was speaking from.
   Questions put by letter — the time you read the question and the place from which the letter was written.

3. Draw the chart using Placidus cusps and following the same procedure as for a nativity.

4. Include the Nodes, the Part of Fortune, and where appropriate the Part of Death or Part of Marriage.

2.
PRELIMINARY CONSIDERATIONS

A question has been asked and the chart has been erected, but no further progress can be made until the Test of Radicality has been applied. A chart may be judged when it is 'radical' or 'fit to be judged'. A non-radical chart should not normally be judged. The following conditions occurring in a horary chart may render it unfit for judgement.

The Ascendant
When the Ascending degree falls between zero and three degrees of any sign, the question is *premature* and judgement cannot be given — it is too early to say. When the Ascending degree falls between twenty-seven and thirty degrees of any sign, the matter has passed beyond the point where judgement can be given — it is too late to say. When a question produces a premature chart, the same question may be asked again at a later date. It often happens that circumstances will have changed in some way so that the position is clearer.

Occasionally the astrologer may feel able to waive these restrictions, particularly when the Ascending degree is powerfully linked with the nativity of the questioner, and especially when that degree corresponds with a natal position which seems connected with the question; as, when in a question to do with marriage, the Ascending degree of the horary chart is the same as the Descending degree of the nativity, or the lord of the seventh house.

Saturn

Saturn conjunct the Ascendant or in the first house damages the question, and a retrograde Saturn when so placed is said to destroy the question. We shall see later how such conditions work out in practice, but it will be found that the matter rarely ends well. Often some misfortune intervenes to render the original question irrelevant.

The Competence of the Astrologer

The seventh house of a horary chart, no matter who or what else it represents, also has dominion over the astrologer. It is the house of the artist. When Saturn appears in the seventh house it reflects upon the competence of the astrologer to give judgement on the matter. It is not safe to pronounce under the ray of Saturn; the advice of the astrologer may be unsound.

This rule may be extended to cover the lord of the seventh house. If it is unfortunate in the sign of its detriment or fall, or generally in a poor condition, the judgement of the astrologer may be at fault. Personally I take little notice of this refinement, but Lilly warns against giving judgement in such circumstances. I have found, however, that when the lord of the seventh is retrograde, the astrologer is often prevented from delivering a judgement to the questioner for some reason.

These restrictions do not apply when the astrologer asks the question himself, for then he is acting as his own astrologer and is not represented by the seventh house or its ruler.

The *Via Combusta*

The degree area extending from 15 Libra to 15 Scorpio is known as the *via combusta*. Tradition states that if the Ascendant or Moon falls between these two points, it is not safe to give judgement, and some authorities hold that any significator falling within this degree area is ineffective. The only exception is the degree of the benefic fixed star, Spica, at 23 Libra; this position is considered most fortunate. Personally I have not found this rule reliable, so I tend to ignore it.

Combustion

A planet is said to be ineffective when *combust* — that is, within 8½ degrees of a conjunction of the Sun; its energy is thought to

be burned up by the Sun's rays. Lilly says that when the ruler of
the Ascendant is combust, 'Neither the question propounded will
take nor the querent be regulated.' I do not believe this to be so
in all cases, and in my experience a combust first house ruler does
not render the chart unfit for judgement. However, combustion
certainly does weaken the planet concerned. The condition is more
serious when the planet is applying to a conjunction of the Sun,
and less serious when separating. There is a tradition which says that
when a planet is *cazimi* — that is, within 17 minutes of a conjunction
with the Sun, it is greatly strengthened. So said the old astrologers,
but there is some disagreement about the validity of the claim, so
one should be guided by experience. A Sun-Moon conjunction (a
New Moon) is highly malefic in horary astrology, particularly when
applying. But the condition does not necessarily prevent judgement.

Sunbeams

When a planet is within 17 degrees of a conjunction of the Sun,
and in the same sign, it is said to be *Under Sunbeams*. This condition
weakens a planet but not as seriously as combustion. In order to
clarify the position allow me to give an example:

Suppose that a question has been asked about the sickness of a
certain party, and assume the party concerned be represented by
the planet Mercury. The astrologer will see the condition of Mercury
as reflecting the condition of the sick person. If Mercury is combust,
within 8 ½ degrees of the Sun, and the aspect is applying, the party
is very weak and seriously ill and his condition is getting worse. If
the aspect is separating, it suggests that although the party is very
sick and weak, the worst is over and his condition will gradually
improve. If Mercury is not combust but Under Sunbeams, within
17 degrees of the Sun in the same sign, the party is slightly sick or
out of sorts, but not gravely ill.

Void of Course Moon

Some authorities maintain that a Void of Course Moon is a barrier
to judgement. This term describes the condition of the Moon when
she is unable to perfect any aspect to which she applies before she
or the planet to which she applies changes sign. This means that
the Moon holds a later degree than any other planet in the chart
with which she is capable of aspect, or that, if another planet does

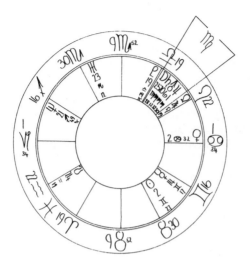

Figure 2.   A Void of Course Moon

The Moon in this chart holds a later degree than any other planet. All her aspects are in the past and she applies to no other body. As she cannot perfect any aspect before she changes sign into Libra, she is Void of Course.

hold a later degree than the Moon, she cannot make aspect with it before that planet changes sign. All the Moon's aspects have been made; all her contacts are in the past; she is applying to nothing. Therefore nothing will happen. Figure 2 is an illustration of a Void of Course Moon.

Where you find the moon void of course, your judgement should be 'Nothing will come of the matter.' If the questioner asks 'Will I get the job?' The answer is 'No, nothing will come of it.' Yet if the question asks 'Is the illness serious?', the answer is the same. Thus a Void of Course Moon allows a judgement. For this reason I cannot agree with the old astrologers that a Void of Course Moon is invariably an unfortunate indication. So far in my experience, charts with the Moon Void of Course could have been correctly answered by saying 'Nothing will come of it.' Lilly frequently judged such charts, and he believed that '. . . the Moon somewhat performs in Taurus, Cancer, Sagittarius and Pisces.'

The Moon is not Void of Course if she applies to Fortuna, and Ivy Goldstein-Jacobson (*Simplified Horary Astrology*) considers that the matter will end well if the Moon applies to Fortuna by parallel within one degree, where she is otherwise Void of Course. Students will know how to calculate the declinations of the planets, and as Ivy Goldstein-Jacobson points out, it is a good idea to calculate the declination of the Moon and Fortuna for every chart erected. An acceptable method of finding the declination of Fortuna is to isolate the day in the ephemeris when the Sun holds the same degree as Fortuna, imagine that Fortuna is the Sun and work out the corresponding declination. You then have the declination of Fortuna.

The Lord of the Hour

Every day of the week is ruled by one of the seven traditional planets; Sunday by the Sun, Monday by the Moon, and so forth. Similarly, every hour of the day has its planetary ruler. The hours between sunrise and sunset and between sunset and sunrise are divided into twelve periods. The first hour after sunrise is ruled by the planet that has dominion over the day (as with the Sun for Sunday). Each period thereafter is ruled by the planet following, in the order: Sun, Venus, Mercury, Moon, Saturn, Jupiter, Mars. The sequence is repeated through the day and night until sunrise the next day, when the planet that has dominion over that day appears as ruler of the first hour.

Astrologers of ancient times believed that a horary chart was not radical unless the lord of the Ascendant and the lord of the hour were of the same triplicity, or agreed in nature. This is not a stricture that modern astrologers apply to their work. In fact, generally, planetary hours have been ignored. Perhaps we have been remiss, perhaps not. When most of the charts in this book were drawn I was not in the habit of noting the lord of the hour. I now note it, but I have not decided yet whether the old stricture is valid. Students who wish to find the lord of the hour for a chart can obtain a planetary hour book from any reliable astrology book supplier.

I have discussed the traditional barriers to judgement above, but sometimes it is most difficult to decide whether a chart should or should not be judged, the testimonies for and against may be finely balanced. It is always wise to err on the side of caution. If you are unsure, defer judgement.

Preparation — Stage Two

1. Apply the Test of Radicality. If any of the following conditions are present in the chart, it is not radical and should not normally be judged.
    (a) The Ascendant located between 0 and 3 degrees of any sign; it is too early to say.
    (b) The Ascendant located between 27 and 30 degrees of any sign; it is too late to say.
    (c) Saturn conjunct the Ascendant or in the first house; the question is damaged, or destroyed when Saturn is retrograde.
    (d) Saturn in the seventh house (except when acting as one's own astrologer); the competence of the astrologer is suspect.
    (e) The Ascendant or Moon located between 15 Libra and 15 Scorpio, the *via combusta,* except for the degree 23 Libra, the benefic fixed star, Spica.

2. Check the Moon to see if she is Void of Course. This condition gives one answer as explained. Do not forget to take account of lunar aspects to Fortuna, including the parallel.

Now refer to Figure 1.

Is the Chart Radical?

You will recall that I asked this question myself after being told of a job opportunity by a friend over the telephone. The chart is drawn for the moment the question formed itself in my mind and for my location at the time.

The Ascending degree is 15 Aquarius, so it does not fall too early or too late in the sign. Neither the Ascendant nor Moon falls within the *via combusta.* Saturn is not in the first house, but he is in the seventh. However, I am my own Astrologer in this case, so the restriction does not apply.

The Chart is Radical and may be Judged

Interestingly, the Ascendant of the horary chart falls almost exactly upon the mid-point of my natal Sun-Midheaven conjunction; thus the tenth house of my nativity is powerfully linked to the horary figure. It is not unusual to find this kind of relationship between the horary figure and the birth-chart. Where possible it is useful to obtain the birth data of the person asking the question so that links of this kind can be recognized and taken into account.

3.
SIGNIFICATORS

The appointment of significators is a crucial part of the process of horary judgement and a more complicated business than may be supposed. I should first make it clear that in horary astrology we give the greater weight to the traditional rulerships. Mars is allowed to rule Aries and Scorpio; Jupiter has dominion over Sagittarius and Pisces; and Saturn holds sway of Capricorn and Aquarius. I do not suggest that the trans-Saturnian planets should be completely ignored, but I see them as suggestive of outer influences over which the querent has little or no control. It will often be found that aspects involving the outer planets seem to back up the indications given by the traditional planets. When selecting significators I always use traditional rulerships, unless the matter under consideration falls very firmly within the influence of one of the three outer planets, or unless one of them figures very powerfully in the chart. If it hits you in the eye it is demanding recognition.

I will divide significators into three classes: (1) primary significators; (2) the Moon; (3) secondary significators.

Primary Significators
The person who asks the question is known as the *querent,* the matter enquired about as the *quesited.* The querent is always represented by the Ascendant of the horary figure, and the ruler or lord of the Ascendant becomes significator of the querent. The house having dominion over the matter enquired about will vary according to the substance of the question, but the ruler of whatever house it happens

to be becomes significator of the quesited. These are the *primary significators.*

Figure 1 is a tenth house question because it concerns the career of the querent. The significator of the querent is Saturn because he is the ruler of the Ascendant sign. The significator of the quesited is Jupiter, because he is the ruler of Sagittarius, the sign on the cusp of the tenth house. In this chart Saturn and Jupiter are primary significators.

The Moon

The Moon is of the utmost importance in horary astrology, as will become evident as we progress. Indeed, it may be said that horary astrology is a lunar art. Allow the Moon to act as co-ruler of every chart; she is as powerful as a primary significator. Whenever the lord of the Ascendant cannot be used for some reason, allow the Moon to substitute and become lady of the Ascendant in her own right. The need for substitution will arise when the same planet rules the querent and the quesited, as in the case of a tenth house question with Virgo on the cusp of the first house and Gemini on the cusp of the tenth house. In such a case the Moon becomes ruler of the querent and Mercury ruler of the quesited.

It is my normal process to treat the Moon as co-significator of the querent in all cases except where she herself happens to be the significator of the quesited. If I cannot find a way to resolve the matter by using the primary significator of the querent, I will try a second reading allowing the Moon to act in place of the primary significator. I am reminded that, according to tradition, the Moon often co-signifies the quesited (a runaway slave from very ancient times, any stray animal, lost object, etc.). Yet I must say that, generally speaking, she seems readily and effectively to accept the role of co-significator of the querent.

The Moon is the fastest moving body in the chart. Aspects she will make before leaving the sign she is in (applying aspects), denote what is going to happen; and aspects she has already made since entering her sign (separating aspects) should describe what has already happened in connection with the matter enquired about. The final aspect of the Moon, before leaving her sign, will give an indication of how the matter will end. She is also an important factor in timing, as we shall see, and it is fair to say that the house occupied by the

Moon frequently reveals the true interest of the querent.

Secondary Significators

I use this term to describe planets which are not primary significators but are important because of their condition in the chart, their nature, or the signs or houses they occupy. For example, if a question about marriage is under consideration, any planet falling in the seventh house of relationships, whether a primary significator or not, must be important. In a question about career, where there are no planets in the tenth house, it may be found that a planet falling in the sign of Capricorn (the natural tenth sign) is important. Also take note of planets having natural dominion over the matter enquired about, such as Mercury for letters and documents, Venus for jewellery, Mars for contests and disputes, etc. Such planets are known as *universal co-significators*.

Figure 1 has a conjunction of Mercury-Neptune in the tenth house of the quesited. This must have some influence in the matter. The sign having natural dominion over tenth house matters is Capricorn, the tenth sign of the zodiac, and the ruler of Capricorn is Saturn. Had Saturn not already been designated as a primary significator through his rulership of the Ascendant, we would take him into consideration as a secondary significator. We should also look for any planets falling within the sign of Capricorn, but in this case there are none. The planets which must be considered when judging this question have now been isolated:

Saturn: lord of the Ascendant and significator of the querent, also lord of the natural tenth sign; a primary significator.

Jupiter: lord of the tenth house and significator of the quesited; a primary significator.

The Moon: Co-significator of the querent, and occupant of the first house.

Mercury-Neptune conjunction: Occupants of the tenth house (the house of the quesited); secondary significators.

Dignity and Detriment

In some circles it is fashionable to play down the importance of the traditional strengths and weaknesses of the planets. In horary astrology, planetary strength or weakness is a major consideration. A planet has dignity or strength when it falls within the sign it rules, the sign of its exaltation, or its natural house. It is weak when opposed to any of these positions. A planet is said to be accidentally dignified when found in an angle, well-aspected, swift in motion, and generally in a good condition. It is an advantage for a planet to be in its own triplicity — that is, in the same element as the sign it rules. When a planet has no strength or dignity of any kind, it is said to be *peregrine* and unable to influence events. Lilly, and the old astrologers, carried the matter of dignity much further by taking account of *terms* and *faces*. Modern astrologers tend to ignore these refinements, but for interest a full table is given in Figure 3.

The House of the Question
There is no problem about identifying the significator of the querent. It is the lord of the ascendant and / or the Moon. But it is not always so easy to determine which house has dominion over the quesited. Is a question about the success or failure of a driving test, a third or ninth house matter? Where the house of a quesited is not clear from the nature of the question, the astrologer must use his skill and experience. He must study the chart and make a decision. You will know which signs and houses control the main departments of life, and you will know the nature of the planets and the matters which come under their influence. So all that remains is to exercise common sense. Frequently the chart itself is of great assistance, and I shall attempt to demonstrate this as we go along. It is most important to learn to bend with the chart and not fight it.

As a general guide I include a broad description of the dominion of the houses, if only because there are a few matters peculiar to horary astrology which come under the control of some of the houses and which need clarification.

As far as the planets are concerned, there are endless lists of matters, persons, animals and plants which traditionally fall under the rulership of the various planets. It is not my intention to repeat them here; whole books dedicated to sign and planetary rulership are readily available. You should know the basic nature of the planets and how they are coloured by the quality of the signs in which they fall, and also whether a planet is regarded as benefic or malefic. Most writers have classified the trans-Saturnian planets as malefic, I do

SIGN	RULER	EXALT	TRIPLICITY DAY	TRIPLICITY NIGHT	DETRIMENT	FALL	TERMS (1–30)					FACES 1°–10°	FACES 11°–20°	FACES 21°–30°
♈	♂	☉	☉	♃	♀	♄	♃	♀	☿	♂	♄	♂	☉	♀
♉	♀	☽	♀	☽	♂		♀	☿	♃	♄	♂	☿	☽	♄
♊	☿		♄	☿	♃		☿	♃	♀	♄	♂	♃	♂	☉
♋	☽	♃	♂	♂	♄	♂	♂	♃	☿	♀	♄	♀	☿	☽
♌	☉		☉	♃	♄		♄	☿	♀	♃	♂	♄	♃	♂
♍	☿	☿	♀	☽	♃	♀	☿	♀	♃	♄	♂	☉	♀	☿
♎	♀	♄	♄	☿	♂	☉	♄	♀	♃	☿	♂	☽	♄	♃
♏	♂		♂	♂	♀	☽	♂	♃	♀	☿	♄	♂	☉	♀
♐	♃		☉	♃	☿		♃	♀	☿	♄	♂	☿	☽	♄
♑	♄	♂	♀	☽	☽	♃	♀	☿	♃	♂	♄	♃	♂	☉
♒	♄		♄	☿	☉		♄	☿	♀	♃	♂	♀	☿	☽
♓	♃	♀	♂	♂	☿	☿	♀	♃	☿	♂	♄	♄	♃	♂

Figure 3. Table of planetary dignitaries.

not think we should be so definite. As I have said, the three outer planets seem to relate to outer influences over which the individual has no control. Sometimes these conditions act for our interest and sometimes against it.

I do not like attaching definite labels to each planet before I have sight of the chart for the question. Each chart is unique, and guided by individual circumstances, the astrologer should apply his own common sense in coming to a judgement.

Figure 3 shows the table of planetary dignities, according to the ancients. The following describes the various dignities of the planets in order of power:

1. *Rulership*. A planet is at its most powerful when occupying the sign it rules.
2. *Exaltation*. A planet is very strong when in the sign of its exaltation, but not quite as powerful as when it occupies its own sign.
3. *Triplicity*. A planet has an advantage in its own triplicity, and it will be noticed that the control of the triplicities varies between day and night. During the day the Sun has control over the Fire triplicity but at night Jupiter takes over. The Earth triplicity is controlled by Venus during the day and by the Moon at night. Air has Saturn for the day and Mercury at night, and Water is controlled by Mars both day and night.
4. *Term*. A planet has moderate strength in its own term. It will be seen from the table how Jupiter has its term in the first 6 degrees of Aries, Venus between the 7th and 14th, Mercury between the 15th and 21st, Mars between the 22nd and 26th, and Saturn in the final 4 degrees; and so on through the signs according to the table.
5. *Face*. The weakest of all dignities is *face*. Mars has its face in the first decanate of Aries, the Sun in the second decanate, Venus in the third, and so forth.

A planet without dignity of any kind is called *peregrine*. It is a wanderer and without influence.

The Dominion of the Houses

First: The querent; his personality and appearance; his general well-being.

Second: Resources; money and movable possessions; trade, investments; loss or gain.

Third: Communications; letters, documents, messages, gossip, rumours and reports; transport, short journeys; brothers, sisters and neighbours.

Fourth: The home; houses and landed property; mines and places under the earth; the grave or final resting place; the mother and family; the end of any matter enquired about.

Fifth: Creativity; children; lovers and love affairs; theatres and all places of amusement; leisure activities; gambling, speculation and competitions.

Sixth: Health and service; sickness and distress; service of all kinds; servants and employees; diet, food and clothing; the working environment; apprenticeship; pets and small animals.

Seventh: Relationships; marriage, the spouse, the partner; contracts and agreements; open enemies and opponents; divorce; theft and thieves; the astrologer, the artist; any undesignated person.

Eighth: Death and regeneration; sex, the possessions of the partner; other people's money; wills and legacies; debt and bankruptcy; inner power and psychic activity.

Ninth: Aspiration; long journeys and voyages; emigration; religion and philosophy; dreams and spiritual experiences; higher education; law and law-suits.

Tenth: Status; the career, occupation or profession; reputation; the father, superior, employer; the monarch; the government, the judge; execution and conviction; whoever is powerful in the matter enquired about.

Eleventh: Friends, hopes and wishes; companions, colleagues, advisors, organizations, societies, clubs; group activities; legislation and legislators; stepchildren; adoption; the dearest wish of the querent.

Twelfth: Misfortune; confinement, restraint, prisons, institutions, hospitals; exile; secret enemies; plots, subversion; assassination, murder and suicide; kidnapping; witchcraft; all acts of self-undoing; large animals.

General Dominion of the Planets

The Sun: The life-force. The Sun symbolizes the creative energy of the universe. It is the point of destiny in any chart, and in horary astrology it has special influence over the life of the querent and his ultimate purpose in this state of consciousness.

The Moon: Response. The Moon represents the ability of the querent to respond and adjust to the challenges of the earthly environment, and this is why it is usually given co-signification over the querent in any horary question. It will give an indication of the way in which an individual is likely to handle the experience which forms the background to the questions posed.

When Sun and Moon apply by good aspect in a horary chart and there is no interference from another body to the perfection of that aspect, the querent is responding directly and positively to the demands of his unique destiny, and nothing may then prevent the resolution of the matter enquired of.

Mercury: Communication. Mercury has general dominion over all matters concerned with human communication.

Venus: Possessions. Venus relates to all manner of possessions, including the physical body, children and relationships. It is a benefic influence.

Mars: Individuation. Mars is concerned with all matters that are connected with the querent's need to stress and express his own uniqueness. It is therefore an important consideration in questions to do with competition or direct individual action. It is associated with that part of human nature which is basically aggressive, and for this reason is seen as malefic.

Jupiter: Aspiration. Jupiter controls all matters connected with the expansion of life experience and the enrichment of life generally. It is the planet of opportunity and usually a most benefic influence.

Saturn: Discrimination. Saturn forces one to face reality, and to temper one's personal aspirations with moral considerations and personal limitation. It is regarded as a malefic and restricting influence, but it is essentially a teacher, although the lessons it produces are often harsh and distressing.

Uranus: Reformation. Uranus is responsible for experiences which disintegrate existing conditions and provide the opportunity for readjusting to new conditions. It often acts dramatically, suddenly and unexpectedly, and in this sense it is often seen as malefic. However, it is a challenging influence and can awaken the individual to potential of which he was previously unaware.

Neptune: Refinement. Neptune tends to refine experience and urges people to achieve greater degrees of psychic and spiritual awareness and experience. It can, however, be deceptive and vague. It is responsible for self-delusion, fearful imaginings and worry.

Pluto: Transformation. Pluto transforms all that it touches. It acts rather like Uranus, suddenly and unexpectedly, and it can destroy prevailing conditions at a stroke and leave a person floundering around completely disorientated. However, it does provide the opportunity for rebirth, so that an individual may rise again like the phoenix from the ashes of destruction.

The last three planets are often symbolic of events directly related to the times in which we live, and as such are outside of the personal control of the querent. The student must use his skill and imagination in relating all these planetary influences to the particular circumstances of the question under consideration.

Notes on the Dominion of the Houses
Notice that I have given the mother to the fourth house and the father to the tenth house: this is controversial. Many astrologers reverse this rulership and give the fourth house to the father and the tenth house to the mother, and I must admit that the old astrologers did likewise. However, while acknowledging that I do not follow traditional practice, I make no apology. My opinion arises from clear experience, and in my heart there is not the slightest doubt that the fourth house is the house of the mother, and the tenth that of the father.

When attempting to decide which house has dominion over the quesited, I strongly urge that you do not immediately seize upon a house and stubbornly hold to it. Give careful consideration to the actual chart, allowing yourself to be guided by it. It may be that a lady asks about a man-friend, someone with whom she has been living for some time. Should he be signified by the seventh house as a spouse, the fifth house as a lover, or even the eleventh house as a friend? You may feel that it should be the seventh, because the relationship is well established and of long standing, but if the chart clearly points to the fifth house, then bow to the wisdom of the heavens. Similarly, if a question is asked about marriage and there are no planets in the seventh house, and the ruler seems to have little connection with the matter, do not be afraid to consider the sign of Libra, and Venus its ruler.

The seventh house is given dominion over an undesignated person. Such a person is someone with whom you have no identifiable relationship. Suppose a news report tells you that a child is missing in suspicious circumstances, and you wish to ask a question about the matter (What has happened to X?). Since you have no personal connection with the child, he must be classified as an undesignated person ruled by the seventh house.

The fourth house rules the End of the Matter enquired about. There are two indications of the way in which any matter might end up: the final aspect of the Moon, as already mentioned, and the condition of the fourth house and its ruler. In each case consider these points as part of your assessment.

Aspects

In horary astrology it is usually only the major aspects that are considered: conjunction, opposition, trine, square and sextile. However, there is strong evidence to suggest that the quincunx (150 degrees) is important, particularly in questions to do with sickness. Minor aspects may be seen as offering confirmation of major aspects, but they are generally ignored. When deciding whether or not the Moon should be classified as Void of Course, minor aspects cannot be ignored.

Orbs of Aspect

What orbs of aspect do we allow the planets in a horary chart? Begin by allowing the same orbs as for a nativity, but we must have maximum flexibility. Applying aspects are the most important because they symbolize what may be expected to happen in the matter enquired about. Often the more telling consideration is whether two significators which are moving towards aspect will perfect that aspect before leaving the signs they occupy, rather than whether they are in generally accepted orbs of aspect to begin with. The Moon, as mentioned, is a special case in horary astrology. She is allowed every aspect she can perfect before changing her sign, no matter how far she is from perfect aspect at the outset.

Retrograde Significators

The retrogradation of the outer planets — Pluto, Neptune and Uranus — is rarely of any consequence in horary astrology. Since we use traditional rulerships, any of the other planets can be a significator of the querent, the quesited or another party involved in the situation to which the question refers. If a significator is retrograde it will reflect the condition of the person or matter enquired about. For example, if a question concerns an item of lost jewellery, and that piece of jewellery is signified by Venus, the fact that Venus is retrograde may be seen as reflecting its condition. Or if a person asks about the wisdom of a certain course of action, and the planet that represents him is retrograde, it could be said that by taking the action contemplated the querent is acting against his normal nature, for his significator is moving against its normal motion. Obviously the way in which we interpret a retrograde significator will vary according to the nature of the question in each case. The above instances are broad generalizations.

Mercury retrograde is more of a special case. When a question produces a retrograde Mercury, it suggests that either: (a) the astrologer is not in possession of all the facts relating to the case, and there is more information to come; and/or (b) the querent may well change his mind about the matter and decide not to pursue it.

It should be said that no matter what planet represents the querent, Mercury will always have something to say about his state of mind when the question was asked. Thus, if Mercury is combust, the querent may be totally lacking in confidence, and when Mercury is Under Sunbeams he will not be very confident. But when Mercury is in the sixth house, particularly when close to the cusp, the querent is usually so worried about the matter that his health is suffering.

Sometimes the question does not accurately reflect the real concern of the querent. A young lady who asks 'Will I ever have a family?' may actually mean 'Am I pregnant?'. The astrologer should always try to ensure that as much is known about the situation as possible at the outset, but the chart can give signs of secrecy. As mentioned above, Mercury retrograde can indicate that there is more information to come; but also when *mute signs* are prominent it can show that not all has been revealed. Mute signs are those of the creatures which lack voice, the Water signs — Cancer, Scorpio and Pisces. Take note of the Ascendant, the Moon and the rulers of the querent and quesited. The more that occupy mute signs the more likelihood there is of secrecy.

Preparation — Stage Three

1. Calculate the major aspects, but include the quincunx. Allow normally accepted orbs; conjunction, opposition, trine and square — 8 degrees; sextile — 6 degrees; quincunx — 2 degrees; but take special note of aspects which will mature within the signs the planets occupy, and allow the Moon every aspect she is able to perfect before leaving her sign.
2. Note cases of combustion, Sunbeams, and retrogradation, especially Mercury.
3. Consider the question carefully and decide what house has dominion over the quesited.
4. Appoint the significators; lord of the Ascendant for the querent, and the lord of the appropriate house for the quesited. Always accept the Moon as co-significator of the querent, except when she is significator of the quesited.
5. Isolate any secondary significators, such as planets falling in the material houses or in the sign which naturally governs the subject of the question, and universal co-significators — that is, planets having natural dominion over the matter enquired about.

The preparation stages are now complete and we may turn to the matter of judgement.

4.
PERFECTION

The object of the astrologer when judging a question is to discover — in the words of William Lilly — 'Whether the thing demanded will be brought to perfection, yea or nay.'

There are five basic ways in which a matter may be brought to perfection. These are hard-tested rules that have come down to us from ancient times.

1. Conjunction: When the ruler of the querent and the ruler of the quesited are applying to a conjunction in the first house or any angle, and meet with no obstruction before perfection of the aspect, the matter enquired about will be achieved. It will be achieved quickly if the significators are swift in motion and strong by sign. It will take longer if the conjunction occurs within succeedent houses, and if cadent, it will take much longer and will not be achieved without difficulty.

2. Sextile and trine: When the principal significators apply to each other by sextile or trine aspect, from positions of strength, and no difficult aspect intervenes before the aspect between the significators is made.

3. Square and opposition: Matters may be brought to perfection when significators apply to each other by square aspect, if both planets are angular, strong by sign, and not retrograde. An opposition between significators can bring matters to perfection, but only at heavy cost, and the querent is likely to regret that the thing was done at all.

4. Translation of light: Translation occurs when the significators

Translation of light (1)
In this example Venus is separating
from a conjunction of Jupiter, but
the Moon approaches first Jupiter
and then Venus by sextile. The
Moon is therefore translating the
light of Jupiter back to Venus, and
invoking again the potency of the
conjunction.

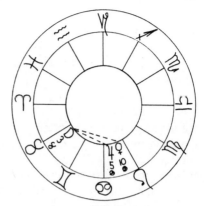

Translation of light (2)
In this example Venus is separating
from a conjunction of Jupiter, but
the Moon is just separating from a
sextile of Jupiter and applying to a
sextile of Venus. The Moon is
therefore translating the light of
Jupiter back to Venus, and invoking
again the potency of the conjunction.

It is this version which I regard as
a true translation of light.

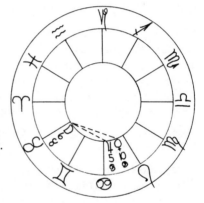

Collection of light
In this example the Moon and Venus
are not in aspect, but both apply to
Saturn. Saturn is therefore said to
collect the light of Moon and Venus,
and may act to bring agreement
between the two.

Figure 4.

of the querent and quesited are separating from good aspect with one another, but a third body, faster in motion than both of them, and in an earlier degree, makes aspect to each of them in turn. The third planet is bringing the influence of the separating aspect back to potency again.

This definition is a modern one and less demanding than the ancient definition. The old definition required that when the significators of the querent and quesited are separating from conjunction, sextile or trine, and some other faster planet *separates* himself from one of the significators — with whom he is in reception by sign, triplicity or term (see below under 'Mutual reception') — and then applies to the other significator by conjunction or aspect before meeting with an aspect of any other planet, he is translating the energy of the one significator back to the other.

5. *Collection of light:* When the significators of querent and quesited are not in aspect, but each makes an applying aspect to a third planet, slower in motion than both of them and in a later degree, the third planet collects the lights of both, and through his influence perfection may be achieved.

As with translation, the old Astrologers required that there should be some form of reception between the significators and the third planet.

I make no further comment upon these basic rules of perfection. They are solid rules of horary astrology and any work upon the subject will enumerate them. As we consider example charts we shall see how they work out in practice. Now I must acquaint you with two other ways in which perfection may be achieved.

6. *Mutual application:* When the principal significators are in incomplete favourable aspect, and one is moving towards the other by retrograde motion, they are *mutually applying* to each other, and it is an indication of success. (This mode of perfection is given by Ivy Goldstein-Jacobson in, *Simplified Horary Astrology*.)

7. *Favourable application of the Lights:* When the Moon applies to the Sun by sextile or trine, and no malefic aspect intervenes before the lights perfect their relationship, this is, in my own experience, a most powerful indication of success — probably the most powerful of all. I have only known this mode of perfection fail when the Sun

or Moon have been involved with malefic fixed stars.

Mutual Reception
When two planets occupy each other's natural sign, they are in
mutual reception. When reading a horary chart we can allow them
to exchange signs so that each planet moves to the sign where it
is most powerful, but they retain their original degrees. Mutual
reception usually allows the querent some kind of choice in the
matter, promises the assistance of some third party, or gives an escape
route from some difficult situation. This relationship is often a strong
aid to perfection, but of itself not a definite indication for success.

Mutual reception as understood by modern astrologers seems
confined to the relationship described above. However, in my
experience, it may be extended to cover the following:

1. two planets in each other's sign (as already stated), e.g., Mercury
   in Libra and Venus in Gemini;
2. two planets in each other's sign of exaltation, e.g., Mars in Cancer
   and Jupiter in Capricorn;
3. one planet in the sign of the other, while the other is in the
   exaltation sign of the former, e.g., Jupiter in Libra and Saturn
   in Sagittarius.

Our astrological forebears went even further, allowing reception by
triplicity, by term, and by face.

So, there are seven main ways of achieving perfection, and mutual
reception can often be of great assistance.

I have already mentioned that the conjunction of Sun and Moon
(the New Moon), is traditionally seen as highly malefic in horary
astrology, and it is particularly difficult when the Moon is applying
to the Sun, but it does not necessarily deny perfection. The French
astrologer, Denis Labouré, considers that the New Moon is too much
for the house in which it occurs to handle, and the great power of
the combustion may produce an abnormality of some kind.

Now we will return to Figure 1. You will remember that we
identified the significators as follows: *primary significators* — Saturn
(ruler of the querent), Jupiter (ruler of the quesited) and the Moon
(co-significator of the querent); and *secondary significators* —
Mercury-Neptune conjunction in the house of the quesited.

Saturn and Jupiter are in incomplete sextile aspect, and although

Jupiter (which is normally faster in motion than Saturn) holds a later degree than Saturn, he is in fact retrograde, so he is moving back towards Saturn and promising to complete the sextile. Here is an example of the sixth of our seven modes of perfection — *mutual application*; but before accepting this testimony of success, we must ensure that Jupiter does actually complete the sextile aspect before turning direct again. The 1977 ephemeris shows that the exact aspect did mature and we can heed its promise. This relationship is made more potent by the dignity of Jupiter in his exaltation sign of Cancer. So we immediately have one strong indication that the thing demanded will be achieved.

The Moon, in the first house, applies to the Sun by trine aspect. She lacks 13 degrees of the exact trine, but as I have already explained, the Moon is allowed every aspect she can make before she, or the planet to which she applies, leaves their signs. As the Moon moves at about 13 degrees a day and the Sun at about 1 degree a day, it is obvious that the trine will be formed before the Sun leaves Scorpio. The Moon applies to nothing but a trine of the Sun, so there is no interference; it is all she has to do, and it will be her final aspect before leaving Pisces. Here is the seventh mode of perfection — an uninterrupted trine between the Lights, and a further indication of success. It is enough. The answer is: Yes, the querent will get the job.

What Happened?
After drawing the chart, I was encouraged by the strong indications of success, so I wrote to the company expressing interest in the position I knew to be vacant. By return of post I received an invitation to call and discuss the matter. I attended for a preliminary discussion on 28 November, but before I left the meeting I had been offered the job and had accepted it. I immediately gave notice to my employers effective 28 December, and after the Christmas holiday I began working for the other brewery. At the time of writing I have had no cause to regret the move.

What about the Mercury-Neptune conjunction in the tenth house? I have not explained it. It is not an easy contact, for Neptune is generally regarded as malefic. It does actually describe quite well my experience with my former employers and my state of mind at the time; but Mercury is about to perfect a conjunction with

Neptune, therefore pointing to something that is going to happen
— what?

It turned out to be a case of confused communications! I had been
offered the job verbally and I had accepted verbally. The company
wanted me to begin immediately after Christmas, so it was necessary
to give my employers notice at once, before I had received a formal
written offer (I had been promised the document within three days).
After waiting ten days I was worried. Telephone enquiries gave me
the assurance that the document was in the post, but it never did
arrive. In the end I called at the company's offices and waited for
the document to be produced. So there was some confusion with
the paperwork (Mercury conjunct Neptune), and for a while I was
worried that I had resigned from one job without definitely securing
the other. As it turned out my worries were unfounded but they
were very real to me at the time.

It is interesting that the exact sextile between the principal
significators — Jupiter and Saturn, occurred exactly at the moment
I ceased officially to be employed by my former company — 29
December 1977 at 00.00 hours.

There are two more points worthy of note in connection with this
chart. Firstly, the Moon and Jupiter are in mutual reception; the
Moon occupies the sign of Jupiter, and Jupiter occupies the sign
of the Moon. I was given the opportunity through a friend, and
Jupiter is lord of the eleventh house of friends. The Moon is co-
significator of me, the querent, and this fact is emphasized by her
position in the first house — my house. If I (the Moon), exchange
signs with Jupiter, as I am entitled to do in cases of mutual reception,
I move from 17 Pisces to 17 Cancer, which is the cusp of my sixth
house. I am thus released from an unhappy and obscure position
(Moon in Pisces intercepted) and allowed to sit powerfully on the
cusp of the sixth house of health and employment. At the same
time I allow Jupiter to go to 5 Pisces in the first house, where its
influence is secretly powerful. The meaning of this reception is, a
friend offered me an opportunity and I benefited by taking advantage
of it. Incidentally, my health improved for two reasons; I was much
happier and my large daily consumption of alcohol ceased.

My final point concerns the fourth house. The fourth house of
any horary chart has dominion over the End of the Matter enquired
about. There are no planets in the fourth house of this chart, but

the lord of the fourth is Mercury. He has two aspects to perfect before leaving Sagittarius: the conjunction with Neptune and the sextile with Pluto. The matter ended with me dissolving my former job (Neptune in the tenth), and achieving a favourable transformation in my career (Mercury sextile Pluto from the tenth).

Notice how we were able to get a clear indication of the outcome from a mutual application between the principal significators, and a favourable application of the Lights. The answer to the question was Yes, twice over. The other indications were relatively minor and in no way interfered with the successful result. Secondary significators often give additional background information, but it is important to remember to give the major weight to the primary significators when making a judgement.

So much for Figure 1.

Figure 5: Will I Stand for Election and Win?
When John asked this question he was a sitting councillor for a district council. It was about five months before the local elections and the fortunes of the Labour Party were at a low ebb. The question is really in two parts. Firstly, 'Will I stand for election?' This concerns the matter of re-selection, because before John could stand for re-election, he would have to be re-selected by his ward committee as a suitable candidate. If he managed to leap that hurdle he would then face the electorate, so the second part of the question demands, 'Will I win?' Let's take the chart through the several stages before judgement.

It is a radical chart, fit to be judged. The Ascending degree is not too early or too late in the sign; Saturn is not in the first or the seventh house, and the Ascendant and Moon are clear of the *via combusta*.

John is the querent, so he is shown by the Ascendant, and his primary significator is Mercury, lord of the Ascendant. Now, what house rules elections — which is the house of the quesited? Status is a tenth house matter because it is the house of reputation, etc., but an election is a competition, and that is a fifth house matter. To some extent the question concerns both tenth and fifth houses. Now here is an example of how the chart itself can be of assistance to the astrologer, for the fifth house is heavily emphasized. The ruler of the querent (Mercury) is in the fifth house; so is Saturn, ruler

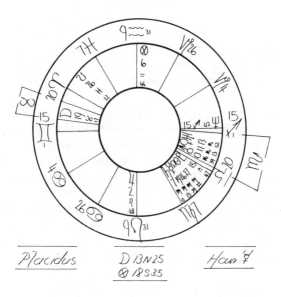

Figure 5. Will I stand for election and win?
20 September 1978 8PM55 GMT 51N46 OW28

of the tenth house of the chart, and the tenth sign of Capricorn.
The Sun is also in the fifth with the North Node. The chart itself
is saying that this is mainly a fifth house matter.

If we accept the advice of the chart and allow the quesited to be
ruled by the fifth house, we have a situation where Mercury rules
both querent and quesited, because Gemini is upon the Ascendant
and Virgo upon the fifth cusp. The Moon now becomes primary
significator of the querent and Mercury is given dominion over the
quesited. Despite this move, Mercury is not completely absolved
of responsibility for the querent; he should still describe the man's
condition, particularly his state of mind. The Sun must be counted
as a secondary significator because he is in the fifth house (which
is the natural House of Leo, in which the Sun may be said to be
'at home'). Saturn must also be regarded as a secondary significator
because his is the ruler of the tenth and upon the cusp of the fifth.
Having dealt with the preliminary considerations, we can now carry
on to investigate the chart and attempt a judgement.

Look to Mercury and you will see that he is applying to a

conjunction of the Sun. Indeed he is within 8½ degrees. He is therefore combust and greatly weakened despite the fact that he occupies his sign of exaltation. This condition betrays a lack of confidence: John is combust and therefore feels weak. However, if we examine the ephemeris we will see that the exact conjunction cannot take place within the sign of Virgo, Mercury does not move fast enough to catch up with the Sun before it moves into Libra, so the actual conjunction takes place within that sign. This greatly modifies the negative effects of the combustion.

The Moon is intercepted in the Twelfth House. This is not a good house: it is generally unfortunate and connected with self-sacrifice, bondage, secret enemies, etc. The Moon by her own nature signifies the public, or in this case the electorate. She is strong because Taurus is the sign of her exaltation. She is almost exactly trine Mercury and she is also applying to a trine of the Sun, that is all she has to do; she makes no other aspect, and the trine with the Sun is her final aspect.

We have two roads to perfection — almost; the significator of the querent (the Moon) and the significator of the quesited (Mercury) are not actually in *applying* good aspect, but their relationship is so close, just 4 minutes of arc, that I am inclined to read it as exact. Then we have a favourable application of the Lights: the Moon strong by sign, to the Sun in the fifth house, the house of the quesited. Yes, he will win: he will be re-selected and re-elected.

Note that the Sun is lord of the Fourth House, and as mentioned, the fourth house has dominion over the end of the matter enquired of. Also the final aspect of the Moon gives an indication of how matters will end up. In each case the Sun-Moon trine promises success.

Council work is a form of public service and requires the sacrifice of much of a councillor's leisure time, so it is not unreasonable to find a twelfth house Moon (sacrifice) applying to a Virgo Sun (service).

I told John that he would be successful, and he got on with preparations for the battles ahead. He was re-selected by his ward committee; then on 3 May 1979, the same day as the general election, he was re-elected to the district council. He won with a good majority; the electorate (the Moon) allowed him to win (Sun in the fifth).

John was successful because:

1. A strong Moon applied by uninterrupted trine to the Sun in the house of the quesited.
2. The significator of the querent was exactly, but for 4 minutes of arc, trine the significator of the quesited.
3. The Moon-Sun trine gave an indication of how matters would end through the Sun's rulership of the fourth house of the chart, and because it was the final aspect of the Moon.

These factors were strong enough to outweigh the disadvantages of Mercury combust, the dubious position of Saturn on the fifth cusp, and the unfortunate nature of the twelfth house Moon. A final point is that the North Node, which is regarded as a benefic, strengthened the Sun by being within a degree of conjunction.

It would not be unreasonable for the student to query my handling of the Moon-Mercury trine. It might be felt that one must accept that the aspect is either *applying* or *separating*, in which case if it is applying then it symbolizes what *will* happen, and if it is separating then it symbolizes something that *has* happened. Why should I be permitted to have it both ways? Such a query would be completely justified, but to explain myself I have to make certain suppositions.

The original question concerned two matters, re-selection and re-election, that was the way the question was put. So the possibilities were: he would or would not be re-selected; and if he was re-selected, he would or would not be re-elected. The significator of the querent (the Moon), had two aspects worthy of consideration: the trine with Mercury and the trine with the Sun. The aspect with Mercury, in my opinion, concerned the matter of re-selection, and the aspect with the Sun the matter of re-election. The fact that the Moon was just separating from the trine with Mercury suggests to me that the querent's re-selection was already arranged. The formalities had not been completed, but he knew he would have the support required on the committee for re-selection. These are not wild suppositions on my part to make the chart fit the situation: I know the querent well, and I had a very good idea of his political standing at the time. In any case, that is what the chart is saying, so that must have been the situation.

Figure 6: Will I Lose My Driver's Licence?
This question was originally put to Sheila MacLeod, who passed it to me for judgement, and I am grateful for her permission to reproduce it here.

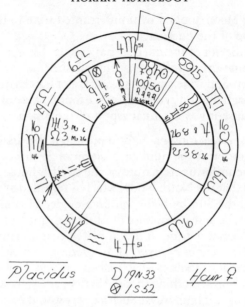

Figure 6. Will I lose my driver's licence?
23 July 1976 2PM21 GMT London

The querent had been summoned for a speeding offence. As it was his third offence within two years and his speed had been excessive, he was in fear of losing his licence. He depended upon his car for a living and was therefore extremely worried.

The chart is radical but the Moon is Void of Course. It is true to say that the Moon has one aspect to make before leaving her sign, a semi-sextile with Jupiter, but we take no account of minor aspects in horary astrology, so she is not quite Void of Course.

We are entitled to expect that any horary chart will describe the condition of the person asking the question. With Scorpio rising, the significator of the querent is Mars. Mars occupies the tenth house in the sign of Virgo, and he applies closely to a square of a first house Neptune in the sign of Sagittarius. We can say that the querent is worried (Neptune) about the effect upon his career (tenth house) if legal action (Sagittarius) prevents him from doing (Mars) his job properly (Virgo — tenth house). So, not surprisingly, the querent is not in a happy condition.

What about the licence — where do we look for its significator?

The planet Mercury has natural dominion over documents (universal co-significator), and so do the sign of Gemini and the third house of the chart. The Moon occupies the sign of Gemini, but she is Void of Course, so she cannot symbolize the licence. We are left with Mercury and Saturn, the former being the natural significator of documents and the latter the lord of the third house. Both are in the ninth house which, among other things, controls legal matters.

Isn't it interesting to find, in a question to do with a legal document, the two possible significators in the legal Ninth House? See how the chart helps the astrologer. As the natural ruler, I considered that Mercury had a better claim to be appointed significator of the licence in this case. Now, as Mercury is separating from Saturn, we can see how this nicely describes a licence marred by previous errors. Venus is important, and the fact that Mercury is about to join her must have some significance. Venus may represent the querent's advisors, for she is lady of the eleventh house of friends and advisors, and since she is placed in the ninth house, we may say *legal* advisors. Mercury is also lord of the tenth house, which is the house of the court. Surely this conjunction must be beneficial.

Remember, the answer to a question which throws up a Void of Course Moon is: 'nothing will come of it.' The querent asks, 'Will I lose my driver's licence?' The astrologer replies, 'Nothing will come of it.' So he will not lose his licence.

Jupiter is angular in Taurus. As lord of the fourth house he rules the End of the Matter, so this argues a happy outcome — but probably an expensive one, because Jupiter is lord of the second house and in the second sign.

My judgement was that the querent would not lose his licence, and that he should delay his court appearance as long as possible, for the further Mercury got away from Saturn (symbolically) the better.

The case was heard on 21 September 1976. The querent did not lose his licence but was heavily fined. In this way does a Void of Course Moon allow a positive judgement.

Note. At the time of this judgement I did not take account of minor aspects when classifying the Moon as Void of Course. Subsequent experience has taught me that minor aspects cannot be ignored.

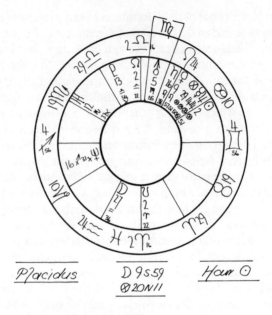

Figure 7.   Is the report true?
24 June 1978 6PM0 GMT 51N46 OW28

Figure 7: Is the Report True?

Before radio, telephone or the penny post, news took a long time to reach various parts of the realm, and quite often, when a report was received, it was later found to be inaccurate. In those days astrologers may well have been kept busy investigating questions similar to this one. Despite the sophistication of modern communications, there are still occasions when it is useful to put such a question.

One glorious summer afternoon I attended a fête in an English village. I was interested to find a lady, a friend of mine, giving Tarot readings from a tent. I knew her to be a serious student of the Tarot with a strong psychic gift. So, throwing caution to the winds, I donated 50p to the cause and exposed myself to a reading. I did not like what I heard, and I emerged from that tent a very worried astrologer. The reading so played upon my mind that when I arrived home I erected a chart for the above question.

It is remarkable how the chart describes the situation. I am represented by Jupiter (lord of the first); she is Mercury (lord of the seventh). The artist, whether Tarot reader, astrologer, medium or whatever, is always shown by the seventh house. See how we sit together in the mysterious eighth house in psychic Cancer. Notice how Mercury is just separating from Jupiter, neatly symbolizing the reading which had just taken place. Neptune in the first shows my worried state, and that is backed up by the Moon separating from an opposition of Saturn.

The Moon is Void of Course in the Third House. This is the house of rumour, gossip, reports, etc. The answer to the question is clear: 'Nothing will come of it.' So the report is not true. A Void of Course Moon in the third house gives an inevitable No to a question of this kind. I ceased to worry. Jupiter is exalted in Cancer. I was more powerful than the artist in this matter.

The reader must forgive my decision not to reveal the details of the Tarot reading, and accept my assurance that nothing did come of it. In this case my Aquarian Sun struggled with my Scorpionic Mars, and Mars won.

Figure 8: Will I Be Promoted This Year?
This question came from a young man anxious to advance his career. He had applied for a better job within his company and was awaiting an interview.

The querent is signified by the Sun (lord of the Ascendant), and the Moon as co-significator; the quesited is signified by Mars (lord of the tenth house of career and status). The primary significators, the Sun and Mars, are in good applying aspect. Before the Sun perfects the trine with Mars, he must make a square with Neptune at 18 Sagittarius. The Moon also applies to Mars by trine, but not directly. She has several aspects to get through before getting to Mars, the most important being a conjunction with the Sun. Both Sun and Moon apply by trine to Fortuna, and the final aspect of the Moon is a conjunction with Venus, lady of the fourth house (End of the Matter), and Venus is strong in the sign of her exaltation.

There are strong indications that the matter will end well, so I judged the querent would be promoted, but with difficulty. The main significators are in cadent houses and Mars is weak by sign. A New Moon, particularly when applying, is traditionally a most malefic indication in a horary chart, and it caused me to harbour

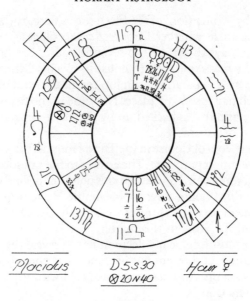

Placidus   D 5 ♋ 30   *Hour* ♀
                          ⊗ 20 N 40

Figure 8. Will I be promoted this year?
8 March 1978 1PM40 GMT London

serious doubts. However, I thought the good aspects strong enough to give the querent his promotion, although I thought the job might prove more demanding than he supposed.

Before either Sun or Moon can complete their promised trine with Mars, each must pass through a square with Neptune. Neptune always seems to produce worry or confusion when in difficult aspect with significators, but I did not consider the Neptunian influence would adversely affect the querent's chances of promotion. Why not? Because Neptune is an 'outer' planet, and I do not consider trans-Saturnian planets to be as powerful or as important as the 'inner' planets in personal matters, unless they are very prominent in the chart.

Notice that the main significators are in Water signs. There is some suggestion of secrecy here: the querent is not revealing all that he might. It may well have been true in this case. I did not find out, but I could use my judgement to speculate upon the cause of the worry symbolized by Neptune in the fifth house if I felt it important.

Mercury is just separating from a conjunction of the Sun. If Mercury had been within 8½ degrees of the Sun he would have been combust, but here he is Under Sunbeams — that is, within 14 degrees of the Sun, and this testifies to a lack of confidence on the part of the querent.

This case does illustrate that a New Moon in a horary chart does not of itself deny success, despite the bad reputation it had with the ancients, because the querent got his promotion. It is true to say that he experienced some difficulty with his new job — he did find it almost too much to handle, particularly at the outset. However, he persevered and is still with it five years later. But then, he is a Sun-Capricorn.

Summary
So far we have examined five questions, all perfected — that is, ended favourably for the querent.

Figure 1: Will I get the job?
Perfection was achieved through: (a) mutual application between the primary significators, and (b) an uninterrupted favourable application between the Lights. The presence of a mutual reception described the assistance of a friend.

Figure 5: Will I stand for election and win?
Perfection was achieved through an uninterrupted favourable application between the Lights, the Moon being strong by sign and the Sun in the house of the quesited. Mercury, a principal significator, was combust, but this did not prevent a successful outcome. However, the actual combustion could not occur without a change of sign.

Figure 6: Will I lose my driver's licence?
In this case we saw the value of a Void of Course Moon. The querent wanted to know if something undesirable was going to happen, and he had every reason to believe that it would. A Void of Course Moon gave the answer: 'Nothing will come of it.' We also saw the successful outcome assisted by an angular Jupiter ruling the End of the Matter, and the natural significator of the matter enquired about (Mercury), applying closely to a conjunction of the benefic Venus. (This case was originally judged as if the Moon was Void of Course.)

Figure 7: Is the report true?
Another example of a Void of Course Moon. The querent was worried about some information he had been given. He wanted to know whether it was true. The Void of Course Moon occurred in the third house of information, etc., and clearly testified that the report was not true, and that nothing would come of it.

Figure 8: Will I be promoted this year?
Perfection was achieved through an interrupted favourable application between the primary significators and between the significator of the quesited and the Moon. Despite the interruption of Neptune and the presence of a New Moon, perfection was not denied, but the indications that the matter would end well were most powerful.

It should now be clear just how important the Moon is in horary astrology. She is co-significator of the querent in the great majority of cases, and all her aspects have significance. Remember that the house or sign she occupies often reveals the true interest of the querent. Planets from which the Moon separates by aspect, and the nature of the contact involved frequently describe what has gone before in the matter enquired about. Planets to which the Moon applies should describe what will happen. Thus we consider every aspect the Moon has made since entering her sign and every aspect she will make before leaving it.

Note every case of mutual reception. The meaning of a reception will vary from case to case, but it often means that the querent will receive the assistance of a third party, or that he is given a way out of an otherwise difficult situation. When allowing the planets involved in a reception to exchange signs, remember they retain their original degrees. The definition of a mutual reception is: *two planets occupying each other's natural sign*. In common with William Lilly, I extend mutual reception to cover planets that occupy each other's exaltation sign, and also when one planet occupies the natural sign of the other, whilst the other planet occupies the sign of the first's exaltation, but such a practice is frowned on by some.

A planet within 8½ degrees of the Sun, and in the same sign, is combust and rendered ineffective unless it is *cazimi*, when it is strengthened. A planet within 8½ degrees of the Sun but in a different sign, or between 8½ degrees and 17 degrees of the Sun in the same or a different sign, is known as Under Sunbeams. It is a weakening influence but far less than a true combustion. When Mercury (indicating the querent's state of mind) or the significator of the querent is Under Sunbeams, it can mean the querent is not in the best of health, or that he is suffering from lack of confidence.

Translation of Light (1)

In this example Venus is separating from a conjunction of Jupiter, but the Moon approaches first Jupiter and then Venus by sextile. The Moon is therefore translating the light of Jupiter back to Venus, and invoking again the potency of the conjunction.

Translation of Light (2)

In this example Venus is separating from a conjunction of Jupiter, but the Moon is just separating from a sextile of Jupiter and applying to a sextile of Venus. The Moon is therefore translating the light of Jupiter back to Venus, and invoking again the potency of the conjunction. It is this version which I regard as a true translation of light.

Collection of Light

In this example the Moon and Venus are not in aspect, but both apply to Saturn. Saturn is therefore said to collect the light of Moon and Venus, and may act to bring agreement between the two.

5.
FIXED STARS AND
IMPORTANT DEGREES

Fixed stars, as you will know, are not really fixed at all; but to us on Earth their movement is so minute that we describe them as such. Actually, fixed stars advance through the zodiac at approximately 50¼ seconds of arc per year. Most natal astrologers appear to ignore the fixed stars completely, but some of them are certainly potent in respect of horary judgements.

When a significator, the Moon or an angle falls within 1 degree of conjunction of certain fixed star positions, the matter in question will be influenced according to the nature of the star concerned.

The main fixed stars considered in horary astrology are listed below together with a brief description of their natures and their approximate zodiacal positions for 1982.

Malefic stars

Algol — 25°55′ Taurus
This star is said to have the nature of Saturn/Jupiter. It is a violent influence and can indicate physical danger. It is popularly referred to as Caput, for it can cause one to lose one's head, literally or metaphorically.

Alcyone — 29°44′ Taurus
Known as the Weeping Sisters, it has the nature of the Moon/Mars. This is a star of sorrow and suggests that the matter enquired of will end in tears.

Vindemiatrix — 9°42′ Libra
This is the star of Widowhood and of the nature of Saturn/Mercury.
It is obviously an important consideration in questions that have
to do with marriage.

Scheat — 29°7′ Pisces
This star is said to have 'malevolence of sublime scope', and appears
to be connected with death, suicide (particularly drowning), bondage
and imprisonment.

Serpentis — 19° Scorpio
This is a strange and potent degree. It has been known since ancient
times as 'the accursed degree of the accursed sign'. It is a tragic degree
of the nature of Mars/Saturn, and I have never known anything
prosper under its ray. When this degree is prominent in a horary
chart, it is enough on its own to destroy the whole matter. Oddly
enough, whatever was responsible for the designation of this degree
as evil in ancient times no longer occupies the degree, but this has
not lessened the traditional maleficity of 19° Scorpio. From a horary
point of view it remains the worst degree in the zodiac. The present
occupant of this degree is the North Scale, and in natal astrology
it is regarded as conferring high intelligence.

Blindness
The following fixed stars are said to be connected with blindness,
and it is unwise to have an operation, or treatment, involving the
sight when these degrees are prominent:
North Asellus   7°17′ Leo
Antares   9°31′ Sagittarius
Acumen   28°27′ Sagittarius
South Asellus   8°28′ Leo
Aculeus   25°31′ Sagittarius
Facies   8°4′ Capricorn

Benefic stars

Regulus — 29°35′ Leo
Known as the Royal Star, of the nature of Mars/Jupiter, it is fortunate
in matters connected with status and leadership.

Spica — 23°35′ Libra
The most fortunate star in the zodiac, of the nature of Venus/Mars.
All matters prosper under its influence.

Wega — 15°4′ Capricorn
This is generally regarded as a fortunate star of the nature of
Venus/Mercury. It is particularly connected with skill and fortune
in politics.

The whole area of the fixed stars requires much study and
experiment, both from a horary and a natal angle. I would
recommend Vivian Robson's book — *The Fixed Stars and
Constellations in Astrology*. Meanwhile the stars listed above are
the most commonly employed in horary astrology.

Critical degrees
There are 28 critical degrees in the zodiac. The determination of
these degrees is based upon the average daily motion of the Moon.
The general consensus concerning these critical degrees in relation
to horary astrology seems to be that when a significator of the Moon
is found upon a critical degree, a crisis is about to break. The matter
enquired about is likely to be resolved quite quickly, one way or
the other, in the manner of the house in which the degree occurs.

Here is another area that would repay investigation. These critical
degrees, otherwise known as *lunar mansions,* are found in Arabian,
Indian and Chinese astrology, and each system gives each mansion
a meaning. For the basic information I again refer you to Vivian
Robson's book.

The critical degrees

In cardinal signs:	0	13	26
In fixed signs :		9	21
In mutable signs:		4	17

6.
DENIAL OF PERFECTION

We have seen that there are conditions occurring in horary charts which assist perfection. Conversely there are other conditions which contribute to the denial of perfection. The following cases seek to demonstrate each of these in turn.

Hindrance and Frustration

Figure 9: Will an application succeed?
This question concerns an application for a job which, if successful, would have resulted in the querent obtaining promotion. The question was framed in a rather guarded way because the querent was not entirely sure that he wanted the job; he was exploring its potential. If the job was offered, he intended to take a separate decision about accepting or rejecting it.

The significator of the querent is Mars. He is weak by sign but in his own eighth house. It is a tenth house question because the main purpose is career advancement, so Mercury is significator of the quesited. The primary significators, Mars and Mercury, are in no meaningful aspect with each other, but Mars will eventually make a sextile aspect with Saturn. Saturn is a secondary significator because he sits in the house of the quesited and his own natural house. He must therefore be influential in the matter.

Look to the Moon as co-significator of the querent, and we see that the first indications are most promising. Her first aspect is a sextile of Mercury, significator of the quesited, and this is one of

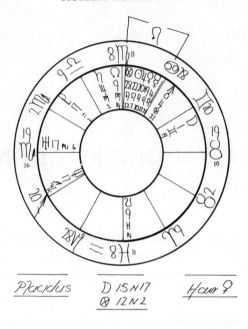

Figure 9.   Will an application succeed? 15 August 1979 1PM07 GMT
51N33 0W06

the accepted modes of perfection. The Moon also applies to a sextile of the Sun, another powerful mode of perfection. The Moon applies well to Jupiter, a benefic and lord of the fourth house, which rules the End of the Matter; and her final aspect is a sextile with Fortuna. It all looks most encouraging.

You will notice that Saturn, in the house of the quesited, has no good aspects. Being a malefic by nature, and having no mitigation, he must be regarded as totally malefic in this case. Now, before the Moon can make her promised aspects with all those planets in Leo, apart from Mercury, she must pass through a square aspect with Saturn. Thus she is hindered; Saturn frustrates her efforts to link with the Leo stellium. This condition is known as *hindrance and frustration*.

In this case the querent had an interview which he considered most promising — Moon sextile Mercury. He was promised a result within three weeks. Three months later he received a letter telling him he had been unsuccessful.

Saturn was too solid a barrier for the Moon to penetrate. He is very powerful in the chart, natural ruler of tenth house affairs, in his own house, and conjunct the Midheaven. Without any good aspects he is a most formidable obstacle. The primary significator of the querent, Mars, is without aspect and weak in mute Cancer, I would call him *peregrine* despite being in the eighth house, because he is completely unable to influence events.

My original feeling about this chart was that the matter would end successfully. I was impressed by the good applying aspects of the Moon, particularly the Sun, and by the uninterrupted applying sextile between the Moon (for the querent) and Mercury (for the quesited). I was wrong. It was a mistake to underestimate the power of an afflicted Saturn in the house of the quesited. His dominant position in the chart must mean something and must influence the matter enquired about.

Finally, I did the unforgivable; I ignored the fact that Serpentis rises. As I have said, I have never known anything prosper under the ray of Serpentis, and really its position at the Ascendant was enough to destroy the matter.

Impedition

Figure 10: Will I marry this one?
Where two significators are in a weak and bad condition, and nothing in the chart assists them, such as mutual reception, they are described as *impedited*, and the matter cannot be brought to perfection.

This question concerns the possibility of marriage, so it is a seventh house affair. Saturn is the significator of the querent and the Sun is for the quesited. The Sun is further emphasized because it falls in Libra, the natural sign of marriage.

In this chart the Sun is in the sign of its fall and therefore weak. It is also contained between two malefics (see Figure 12), Pluto and Uranus. Saturn is also in the sign of his fall and close to the malefic South Node. So both the primary significators are weak, and they have no relationship with each other. Nothing in the chart can bring them together. The chart is impedited; the answer to the question is No.

Apart from the poor condition of the primary significators, Venus the natural ruler of marriage is conjunct Neptune at the Midheaven,

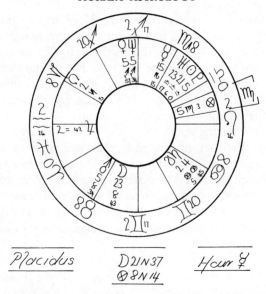

Placidus   D 21N37   Hour ♀
                ⊕ 8N14

Figure 10. Will I marry this one? 14 October 1973 2PM43 GMT
50N27 3W33

casting a ray of confusion (Neptune) and rashness (Sagittarius) over
the whole matter. Also, the chart is not radical, because less than
three degrees rise at the Ascendant; and finally, as if to remove any
vestige of doubt, the Moon is Void of Course and therefore nothing
will come of the matter.

Never allow yourself to be seduced away from basic considerations
by something like Jupiter rising. In this case all it seemed to mean
was misplaced optimism. The querent did not marry 'this one', and
the relationship gradually petered out.

Refranation

Figure 11: Will she collaborate with me?
I was engaged upon an astrological project. I knew that a friend —
a young lady — was sympathetic to my work, and I admired her
astrological skill. At a certain moment I was moved to ask her to
collaborate with me and produce the end-product jointly. I noted
the time the question formed itself in my mind and a few minutes
later I made the proposition. She noted the time I approached her,

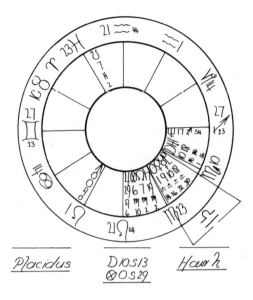

Figure 11. Will she collaborate with me? 24 September 1979 9PM24 GMT London

and then we went our separate ways and studied our respective horary charts. Such is the way of astrologers. When I had a chance to look at my chart I knew she would refuse, and from her chart she knew she must refuse.

My significator is Mercury (appropriate, for it is the ruler of my nativity). Now, the young lady could be shown by the seventh house (alliance), or by the eleventh house (friend). Really she is a mixture of both, but as Jupiter rules both houses, her significator is not in doubt. I am shown in Libra in the fifth house, engaged in creative writing — Mercury conjunct Venus in Libra; and the young lady is placed close to the I.C. upon the degree of the benefic fixed star, Regulus.

You will see that our significators lack 19 degrees of exact sextile aspect, but eventually the aspect will perfect, and that suggests a coming together. However, the sextile aspect cannot form before Jupiter leaves the sign he occupies. This condition is known as *refranation.* Perfection is denied because the significators cannot meet from the signs they inhabit. Even if Mercury could aspect Jupiter before he moved into Virgo, the perfection of the aspect is interrupted by Pluto. Mercury must conjunct Pluto (malefic) before getting to Jupiter, so we have *hindrance and frustration* as well as *refranation*. Pluto here may well symbolize a third party who intervenes to frustrate the querent's aims.

If we look at the Moon as co-significator of the querent, we see that she is applying to Jupiter by square aspect. It has already been mentioned that it is sometimes possible to achieve perfection through square, but the planets concerned must be angular or strong by house (which Jupiter is), and/or strong by sign (which neither is). Indeed the Moon is weak in Scorpio, and in the *via combusta*, which tradition says should render her ineffective. This aspect is not denied by refranation, because the Moon can catch Jupiter before he moves into Virgo. However, the pattern is not strong enough to allow perfection by square. In any case the Moon would have to conjunct Uranus and sextile Saturn before relating to Jupiter — more hindrance, more frustration.

Finally, the chart is not radical because the Ascending degree falls just within the last three degrees of Gemini.

So far, excellent friendly relations have continued, but no collaboration has occurred.

Besiegement and Duress
When the Moon or a significator is positioned between two malefics, it is *besieged*. It is a condition that restricts the ability of the person signified to move in the matter enquired about. It is indicative of pressure or harrassment; the person is trapped between two evil influences. It does not matter how far away the malefics are — the besiegement still applies. But the closer the malefic planets are to the significator, the more serious and intense the evil influence. When the besiegement is very close, the person concerned is said to be *under duress*.

Figure 12: Shall I sell my ICI shares?
This question was put to me by Sheila MacLeod and it appears with her permission. It was asked against the background of a serious national financial crisis, and in the light of an opinion given by another astrologer that the stock market was in imminent danger of collapse.

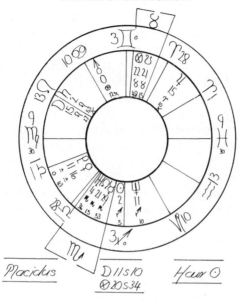

Placidus   D 11 s 10   H cusp O
                ⊕ 20 S 34

Figure 12.   Shall I sell my ICI shares? 24 November 1975 11PM50 GMT
London

The querent's significator is Mercury. It is in the third house in
the final degrees of Scorpio, and it can make no aspect before
changing sign. It is also Under Sunbeams, being within 17 degrees
of the Sun. The querent's condition is one of lack of confidence
about the safety of her investment, because of the reports (Mercury,
third house) she has heard.

The quesited is movable property and is therefore under the control
of the second house, which is ruled by Venus. Venus is also universal
co-significator of financial matters, so she is powerfully placed in
her own house and dignified in her own sign of Libra. This strong
position testifies to the inherent value of the investment, but Venus
has just entered the *via combusta* and is, for the moment, ineffective.
She is also besieged by Uranus on one side and Pluto on the other.
Thus the investment itself is under pressure and unable to move
without incurring the wrath of the malefics.

In view of the weakness of Mercury, we must give our main
attention to the Moon as co-significator of the querent. She applies
by close sextile to Venus. However, she is fixed and cadent and also

besieged by two malefics — Saturn and Pluto. Saturn is very close, so the querent is under duress. She is worried by the prevailing financial climate and by the reports she has heard.

How do we go about judging such a chart? The querent asks whether she should convert some blue-chip shares into cash. The chart is telling us that those shares are a good investment because Venus is strong and dignified, but for the moment they are afflicted by conditions which any individual is powerless to influence because Venus is besieged by outer planets and about to pass through the *via combusta*. The querent herself in the shape of the Moon is also afflicted, by a combination of Saturn and Pluto. She is in good aspect to her investment, but any move by her or her investment can only be made under the shadow of the malefics which afflict each significator.

My judgement to the querent, who is also an astrologer, was as follows:

The Moon cannot move in this matter without stirring up a reaction from the malefics which afflict her. Certainly she is in trine with Jupiter, but that is a separating aspect and Jupiter is retrograde. Venus has just entered upon her Test of Fire in the *via combusta,* and she has just passed the point (separating opposition from Jupiter), where she is as far from expansion as she can possibly be. From now on Venus, the investment, will get steadily closer to expansive Jupiter, although she has to run a few gauntlets on her way.

At the base of the chart is gold (the Sun), in expansive Sagittarius. It is held for the moment by Saturn, but the good aspect emphasizes the long-term value of the investment. With the Moon in such a difficult position and half-way through a fixed sign it is not the time for action in the matter. Do not sell — you would only be changing the form of your assets, and at the moment I would sooner have a tiny stake in ICI than a wallet full of pound notes. Progress the Sun a day for a year until it reaches Neptune — inflationary Neptune of drugs and chemicals: there sits ICI. If you like, sell then.

It is worth reflecting that the twelfth house is said to have dominion over the subconscious. The Moon in this chart sits in the twelfth house in a fixed sign; subconsciously the querent may not have wanted to sell her shares because they were inherited from her father.

This example is a useful indication of how I regard the outer planets. In this case they were besieging the significators, and I saw them as being representative of the national financial crisis then in operation. This crisis had reached into the personal affairs of the querent and she was powerless to influence events.

Summary
These last four examples illustrate the main causes leading to denial of perfection.

Figure 9: Will an application succeed?
Perfection was denied because the Moon was unable to complete her good applying aspects without first encountering a difficult aspect with Saturn. Saturn hindered the Moon and caused frustration to the querent.

Figure 10: Will I marry this one?
In this case both the main significators were weak by sign and not in aspect with each other, they were impedited and perfection was therefore denied. The Moon was not applying to any significator: she was Void of Course, and she was also besieged between Mars and Saturn.

Figure 11: Will she collaborate with me?
The main significators, Mercury and Jupiter, were not actually in aspect, but because Mercury moves faster than Jupiter, an aspect would eventually occur. However, the relationship could not mature before Jupiter moved from Sagittarius. Perfection was denied by refranation. Mercury was also hindered by Pluto.

Figure 12: Shall I sell my ICI shares?
The significators of both querent and quesited were besieged on either side by malefics. They could not move without attracting evil influences. Besiegers often represent conditions or circumstances beyond the control of the querent.

You will notice that in each of these examples the restrictive condition I was seeking to illustrate was not the only evidence to suggest that perfection would be denied. This happens more often than not — a pattern emerges that seems to point to either perfection or denial. Most horary charts are capable of considerable expansion to take account of the frequently intricate circumstances surrounding the question and the life of the querent. Always study the chart carefully and try to build up a picture of the life situation which provoked the question.

7.
THIRD-PARTY QUESTIONS

So far we have considered only questions put directly by the querent to the astrologer about some aspect of his own affairs, but very often a person will ask a question about the affairs of another. In such cases we must decide which house rules the person who is the subject of the question, and which house has dominion over the area of his affairs enquired about. If the question for Figure 1 had been 'Will my brother get the job?', I would have identified as follows:

I asked the question, so I am shown by the Ascendant of the chart, and Saturn is my significator. My brother must be shown by the third house, because it is the house of brethren. The third house has Taurus at the cusp so Venus is the significator of my brother. My brother's career is shown by the twelfth house of the chart. Why? Because, as my brother is shown by the third house, in order to arrive at the house of his career, we must count ten houses from the third cusp (not forgetting to count the third cusp as his first house), and by this process we arrive at the twelfth house of the chart. Capricorn is on the cusp of the twelfth house, so Saturn becomes the significator of my brother's career. If the question were about his wife (my sister-in-law), we would count seven houses from the third in order to arrive at the house of his wife. If the question were about his son, we would count five houses from the third to bring us to the house of his children, and so on.

It really is a simple matter to work out which House rules which person. Just use your common sense. Which house rules a maternal

grandmother? She is the mother of the mother, and as the fourth
house (I would say) rules the mother, the fourth from the fourth
rules the mother's mother. Which house rules a paternal grandfather?
He is the father of the father, and as the tenth house (I would say)
rules the father, the tenth from the tenth rules the father's father.
So the seventh house rules a maternal grandmother and the fourth
house a paternal grandfather.

A friend is shown by the eleventh house, a lover by the fifth house,
and an undesignated person by the seventh house. An *undesignated
person* is someone with whom the querent has no relationship,
someone who will not conveniently slot into any other house. Let
us suppose I hear a news report about a missing child and I am moved
to ask the question 'What has happened to X?' Since I have no
relationship with the child, he/she is a undesignated person and
belongs to the seventh house. In a general sense anyone 'opposing'
the querent is also signified by the seventh house. If the querent
is the loser of property, the thief is shown by the seventh house.
If the querent is an interviewee, the interviewer is shown by the
seventh. If the querent is a patient, the doctor is of the seventh house
— and so on.

When a question is received about the affairs of a third party,
it is a good idea for the beginner to turn the chart so that the house
of the person enquired about becomes the Ascendant. The chart
may then be read as if that person had asked the question himself.

Figure 13: Will my sister pass her driving test?
This chart was produced in one of my astrology classes. One of the
members had asked a question about the affairs of her sister. She
drew the chart at the moment the question occurred to her, but
no time was recorded. This is not one of my judgements: the lady
had already given a judgement and the result was known. The chart
as it stands, Chart 'A', nicely reflects the situation. The Sun is in
the third house (sisters and communication), the Moon is in Gemini
(the sign of communication), and the Moon closely applies by trine
to the Sun. However, let us turn the chart so that the house of the
sister becomes the Ascendant of the chart. We may then read the
chart as if the sister had asked the question. Chart 'B' is chart 'A'
turned.

Four bodies have a close association with the sister; Mars, because

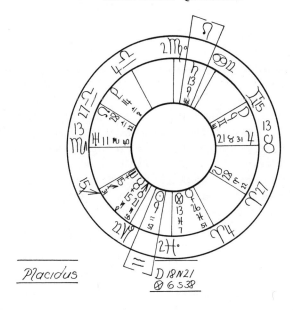

Placidus

Figure 13a. Will my sister pass her driving test?
29 January 1977 E. London (no time noted)

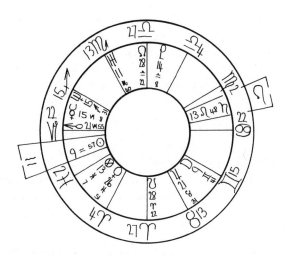

Figure 13b. The above chart turned to show third cusp rising.

he is conjunct the Ascendant; Saturn, lord of the Ascendant; the Sun, occupant of the First House; and the Moon — co-ruler of the chart.

This is a third house question because it is concerned with communication, and the chart confirms this by placing Mars, lord of the third house, upon the Ascendant in the sign of his exaltation, thus powerfully stressing his importance. So Mars is the ruler of the quesited, but he has no relationship with the Sun, Saturn or the Moon. This is not very encouraging, but we must not be put off because the chart contains several indications of success.

There is the potent conjunction between the Ascendant (which symbolizes the sister) and Mars — the lord of the quesited. See how Mars is just separating from a trine of Jupiter. Then Mercury, who is faster in motion than both of them and in an earlier degree, will make aspect to each of them in turn. This may be claimed as a *translation of light*; Mercury is translating the light of Jupiter back to Mars. Also, we have the Moon in the fifth house and the sign of communication applying closely to the Sun by trine in the first house, and nothing interrupts the completion of the aspect. There is promise of success from two modes of perfection; a translation of light and an uninterrupted good applying aspect between the Lights.

What about Saturn in the seventh house and the applying opposition from the Sun? The Sun and Saturn are in mutual reception, and this is a harmonious and helpful condition. The sister will take a driving test. She is shown by the first house; the test examiner comes under the dominion of the seventh house. The Sun in the first house may act as one of the significators of the sister; Saturn in the seventh may act as the significator of the examiner. Since they *receive* each other they are in agreeable relationship, clearly they hit it off together.

I have noticed that in questions to do with luck, elections, competition, examination, etc., the fifth house is usually important. We have already noted the positions of Jupiter and the Moon in the fifth house, but the ruler of the fifth is Venus, and she is in her own second house and in the sign of her exaltation. Both Mercury and Mars are in sextile aspect with her. Indeed Mercury translates light between Jupiter and Venus as well as Jupiter and Mars.

Finally, apart from Mars being ruler of the quesited, he also has dominion over the End of the Matter through his control of the fourth house. The End of the Matter was that the facility to drive (Mars), was given to the sister (Mars conjunct the Ascendant). She passed her test.

Doubtless you will have noticed that the original chart has its Ascendant just within the *via combusta*, and the turned chart has Saturn in the seventh house. These conditions have already been mentioned as affecting the radicality of a question. Personally, I usually ignore the *via combusta* rule, and when Saturn is the significator of the person about whom the question is asked, or of the quesited, he should not be counted as a malefic.

I should mention that third-party questions do not affect the positions of Fortuna or any other 'Parts'. They are calculated on the original chart, so they hold the same degree in both charts.

Horary questions may be broadly divided into four categories:

1. *Personal questions:* Questions put of the querent directly to the astrologer about some aspect of his own affairs. Examples: Will I get the job? When will I marry?

2. *Related third-party questions:* Questions put by the querent about the affairs of another with whom he has some form of relationship. Examples: Will my brother get the job? Will my friend recover?

3. *Unrelated third-party questions:* Questions put about the affairs of someone with whom the querent has no relationship. Examples: When will Prince Charles marry? Will Carter be re-elected President of the USA?

4. *General and philosophical questions:* Questions concerning the interest of the mass of the people, or questions having to do with some philosophical matter. Examples: Will a cure be found for Cancer? Will Britain suffer nuclear attack? What is horary astrology? What is the nature of karma?

Most students of astrology find it quite easy to accept the validity of the first two categories, but there is often difficulty in accepting that any individual has either the right or the competence to ask questions falling under the last two categories. A frequent objection demands what mandate the astrologer or any querent has to ask such questions.

It is my personal view that if a question is put with good heart and from sound motives, and if the chart is radical, you have the astrologer's mandate to pose or judge any question. I firmly believe that this form of divination is self-regulating. If you have no right to judge a certain question, its resolution will be denied you through the chart itself. The only restriction to judgement is one's own sensibility and the actual horary figure.

My next two examples are illustrations of questions falling within the third category.

Figure 14: Will Kennedy become President of the USA?
I asked this question shortly after I heard that Edward Kennedy had declared his intention of running for the Presidency of the United States. Kennedy and I have no relationship with each other. He is therefore an *undesignated person* and under the dominion of the seventh house. This chart has been turned so that the seventh house becomes the Ascendant.

Kennedy is signified by Saturn and sits appropriately at the Midheaven. There he is aspiring to the most exalted office in his country. It is a powerful placing for Saturn, angular and in his natural house. This is clearly a tenth house question, so Mercury is the significator of the quesited, but since elections are involved, the fifth house should also be considered, with its ruler, Mars.

Mercury, lord of the tenth, occupies the final degrees of Scorpio and is separating from a sextile of Saturn. This promises nothing. Saturn is so strong, however, that we must see if any other body can tap his power. Venus applies very closely by sextile from the eleventh house, but she is weak by sign. The Moon is of great importance here, because apart from her role as co-ruler of the chart, she naturally symbolizes the public or electorate. The Moon's only applying aspect is a square with Mercury, but even that aspect is denied by refranation, because Mercury moves into Sagittarius before the Moon can catch him. The Moon is effectively Void of Course. Nothing will come of the matter. The chart says that Kennedy will not become President.

Despite strenuous efforts by his friends to get him nominated by the Democratic Party Convention, he was not successful. His friends are shown by the eleventh house, which is ruled by Venus. This explains the Venus/Saturn contact, but their lack of power is

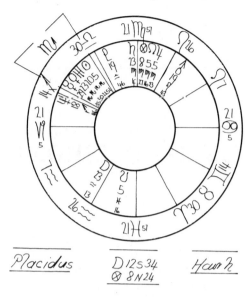

Figure 14. Will Kennedy become President?
29 October 1979 9PM02 GMT 51N46 0W28

betrayed by the weakness of Venus in Scorpio. Mars rules the fifth, he makes no aspect with Saturn, and although he applies by sextile to Pluto in the tenth, he then immediately makes a square with the eleventh house Uranus, another indication of the failure of Kennedy's friends.

8.
MULTIPLE QUESTIONS

It sometimes happens that a querent will pose more than one question at the same time. The questions themselves may not be related. It is possible for an astrologer to resolve several separate questions from the same horary figure, but he must make a distinct approach to the chart on behalf of each question, and he must take care to clear his mind of one set of circumstances before considering another set. The next two cases are illustrations of multiple questions.

Figure 15: (1) Will my wife be safely delivered of a healthy child?
          (2) Will contracts be exchanged?
These questions came from a worried expectant father. He was concerned about his wife because she was most displeased at finding herself pregnant, and he was rather depressed by it all. In preparation for his expected family, he was negotiating the purchase of a house, but matters had been delayed and he was afraid that the deal would fall through.

The wife is represented by the seventh house of the chart. The Moon is conjunct the seventh cusp, and Mars, ruler of the seventh, is conjunct the tenth cusp. The Moon applies to Mars by square aspect. If the seventh house represents the wife, then the tenth becomes her fourth house, and the Moon, ruler of her fourth, is in her first. With the wife's significator in her fourth, and the ruler of her fourth in her first, and bearing in mind the prominence of those significators at the angles, and the association of Moon/Cancer/fourth house with motherhood, it is an understatement to say that

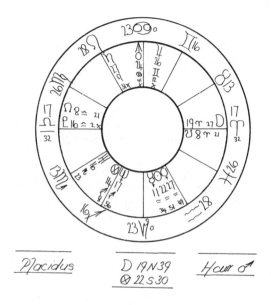

Figure 15.
(1) Will my wife be safely delivered of a healthy child?
(2) Will contracts be exchanged?
11 February 1978 10PM15 GMT 51N46 0W28

the chart fairly reflects her condition. The Moon applies to Mars in the fourth, so she was about to enjoy the experience of motherhood. I was not altogether pleased with the retrograde condition of Mars, but I took this to explain the unpopularity of the pregnancy with the mother-to-be.

Allright, the chart describes the condition of the querent's wife, but will she be safely delivered?

The aspect which symbolizes the approaching state of motherhood is the Moon applying by square to Mars. This is where we must look for the perfection of the matter. Perfection by square is possible in this case because both significators are angular. Any difficulty which the square might provoke is superseded here because the Moon and Mars are in mutual reception, a helpful and beneficial influence. I concluded that the child would be safely delivered.

Now we must consider the child itself. Children are of the fifth house. The lord of the querent's fifth house is Saturn; see how Saturn is at the cusp of the wife's fifth house (the eleventh of the chart). The ruler of the wife's fifth house is the Sun; see how the Sun is approaching the cusp of the querent's fifth house, and is not such symbolism remarkable? Both bodies are weak by sign and the Sun applies to an opposition of Saturn. If the condition of these significators causes any misgivings, forget them, for we have another mutual reception; the Sun and Saturn receive each other, and this augurs well for the child. The querent's wife will be safely delivered of a healthy child.

Should the slightest doubt remain about the happy outcome of the matter, the following testimonies will settle the mind. The sign having natural dominion over children is Leo, and the ruler of that sign is the Sun. The Sun applies well to Jupiter, and the Moon applies by sextile to the Sun. It is the Moon's first aspect and of itself a mode of perfection. The Moon also applies well to Jupiter, to Saturn (lord of the fourth house — End of the Matter), and her final aspect is a sextile with Venus (ruler of the querent). The indications of success are about as impressive as you can get. I judged that all would be well, and because the main significators were in masculine signs, I thought the child would be a boy. As it turned out, a healthy *daughter* was subsequently born to the couple — which just goes to show that the astrologer shouldn't try to be too clever. I was not asked about the sex of the child. I had no mandate therefore to make judgement upon the matter.

Having resolved the first question, we must put it completely from our minds and concentrate upon the second question: Will contracts be exchanged?

The querent is the buyer and represented by the Ascendant. The seller must therefore be shown by the seventh house. Venus is significator of the querent, and Mars significator of the seller. These two are in no meaningful aspect with each other. We must allow the Moon as co-significator to act for the querent, and she applies to Mars by square, but there is mutual reception, so the buyer and the seller will agree.

The querent's fourth house is the house of the quesited — property, but the tenth house of the chart represents the home of the seller because it is the fourth house from the seventh. See how the seller (Mars) sits in his own house retrograde, suggesting that he is unable to move out of his home for the time being. Meanwhile the significator of the querent (Venus) is in his own home but just about to change into the fifth house of the chart; this symbolizes an imminent change of residence.

The delays regarding exchange of contracts may be seen through Jupiter in Gemini (legal documents), in the Ninth (legal) house, retrograde.

The eventual success of the matter is not in doubt: Moon/Mars mutual reception, Moon applying well to Saturn — lord of the fourth, and the Moon applying to the Sun by sextile.

I judged that matters would begin to move again with the direct motion of Jupiter on 20 February, and that the house would belong to the querent within eight weeks, and so it proved.

Figure 16: A lady from Cyprus being in the process of divorce asks:
(1) Will I receive a satisfactory property settlement?
(2) Will I retain custody of my children?
(3) Will I remarry my first husband?

I met the querent by previous arrangement at the home of her friend who acted as translator. The lady was being divorced by her husband. She didn't seem particularly upset by it, but she was anxious not to lose the marital home, and she wanted to retain custody of her children. I discovered that the lady had first married many years ago in Cyprus, but the marriage had ended in divorce after a few months. She came to England and married again, and it was this second marriage that was in the process of dissolution. It soon became apparent that her main concern was whether she would remarry her first husband, who was resident in Cyprus.

The property settlement

Libra ascends, close to the degree of the benefic fixed star, Spica; so the querent's significator is Venus. She is positioned in Gemini in the ninth house. This condition emphasizes legal matters and the closeness of the applying square from the Moon suggests that proceedings are imminent.

The querent wishes to retain the marital home. From where she sits in the ninth house she trines Fortuna in the fourth house of property, and she applies by sextile to Saturn, lord of the fourth house of property. The Moon about to perfect a square with Venus

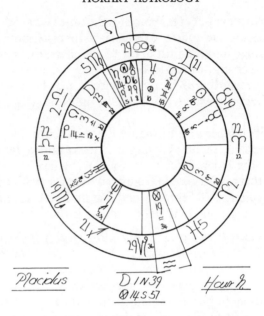

Figure 16.
(1) Will I receive a satisfactory property settlement?
(2) Will I retain custody of my children?
(3) Will I remarry my first husband?
17 May 1978 4PM27 GMT London

(legal proceedings), afterwards makes a trine with the Sun in Taurus. I judged that she would retain her house.

It is interesting that Mars, significator of the husband, is applying to a conjunction of Saturn (the house). He appears to be attempting to get hold of it, but the Part of Marriage gets in the way. In any case Saturn is strong in his own house and Mars applies to an opposition of Fortuna in the fourth, and all this occurs in the house of the court, so the husband's attempt to gain possession will be unsuccessful.

Custody of the children

The children come under the dominion of the fifth house and are ruled by Jupiter. In this country it would be most unusual for the courts to award custody of the children to anyone but the mother unless it was clearly not in their interest. Jupiter is exalted in his own ninth house. There is no indication that the Court will do other than follow traditional (Cancer) practice. I judged that she would retain custody of her children.

Remarriage to the first husband

Where do we look for the significator of the first husband? The Moon occupies the eleventh house of hopes and wishes. After the Moon completes her square with Venus, the only other aspect she makes is a trine with the Sun. So the querent's dearest wish could be that, after her divorce (symbolized by the Moon square Venus), she might remarry her first husband (with whom she had contact although he was resident in Cyprus). Therefore I will make the Sun significator of the first husband. I am encouraged in this view by the fixed nature of the Sun in Taurus suggesting stability and faithfulness. So the significators for this part of the question are: the Moon for the lady and the Sun for her former husband.

She applies to him by trine and that is the final aspect of the Moon. A further indication of success in her objective could be the mutual reception between Mercury/Venus, Mercury, lord of the eleventh house and Venus, lady of the querent. The querent then, has the opportunity of moving from 25 Gemini to 25 Taurus (when planets swap signs through reception they retain their original degrees), and this would produce a very close conjunction with the Sun (significator of the first husband) — success? Not quite, for if the querent took this opportunity and made the move, she would find herself not only combust, but upon the degree of the malefic fixed star, Caput Algol.

There is another approach. The Moon and Mercury occupy each other's signs of exaltation. (I count this as a reception.) If she exercises her choice through the Moon, and ends up on the 23rd degree of Taurus, she would apply closely to a conjunction with the Sun, which is a most malefic condition for the Moon, with or without Algol.

This situation appealed to my romantic spirit. I would have liked to encourage the lady in her venture, but I could never advise anyone to pursue anything which had its end upon Caput Algol. By moving from her present position — Venus, trine Ascendant (Spica), trine Fortuna, sextile Mars, sextile Saturn — she would, symbolically at least, be moving back in time and circumstance and all her hopes and wishes would dissolve under the malefic influences she would contact. I was obliged to advise against the project.

I have no idea of what happened in this case — I have had no contact since that one consultation. It is, however, worth noting that a few years ago Turkey invaded Cyprus, to the detriment of the Greek Cypriots. If she was in Cyprus at the time, who can say how her affairs may have been affected by that event?

Mutual reception can warn against a dangerous course of action.

9.
TIME AND DISTANCE

Questions will arise which contain an element of time or distance, as when a querent asks when a certain event will occur, or where a certain thing or person is located.

Timing
The Moon is the principal agent in timing. The length of time that will pass before a thing demanded will occur is calculated according to the quality of the house and sign occupied by the Moon, and the number of degrees distant she is from an aspect with the significator of the quesited. Each degree of lunar motion equates with a day, week, month or year, according to the following table which is known as — 'The generally Accepted Measure of Time'.

The Moon in	and angular house	= Days
a cardinal sign	and succeedent house	= Weeks
	and cadent house	= Months
The Moon in	and angular house	= Weeks
a common sign	and succeedent house	= Months
	and cadent house	= Years
The Moon in	and angular house	= Months
a fixed sign	and succeedent house	= Years
	and cadent house	= indeterminable period

Thus, if the Moon is in the seventh house (angular) and Taurus (fixed) each degree of her motion is equal to one month. If she is in the

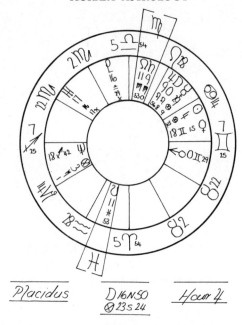

Placidus   D 16N50   Hour 4
                ⊗ 23 s 24

Figure 17.
When will I get a council flat?
26 June 1979 6PM05 GMT Hampstead

eighth house (succeedent) and Scorpio (fixed), each degree of her
motion is equal to one year. If the Moon is in the ninth house (cadent)
and Leo (fixed), it is not possible to calculate the length of time
involved.

Figure 17: When will I get a council flat?
The querent occupied private rented accommodation in north-west
London; it was expensive and conditions were very bad. She was
on the waiting list for a council flat but had no immediate hope
of getting one. In a fit of desperation she posed the above question.

   The querent is signified by Jupiter — lord of the first house, and
the flat by Mars — lord of the fourth house. Mars applies widely
to a sextile of Jupiter, so there is promise of success, but you will
notice that Mars applies to Saturn by square as well as Jupiter by
sextile, and he will pass through a square of Saturn before aspecting
Jupiter. This smacks of hindrance and frustration. We could not

promise success upon this aspect, but there is another route to perfection.

The Moon applies to a conjunction of Jupiter, and she does not have to pass through a hard aspect with Saturn to get there, so here is another more direct promise of success. One could reason that, as the Moon is natural significator of fourth house matters, the flat is coming to the querent. Now the Moon is in a succeedent house and a fixed sign, and the Generally Accepted Measure of Time appropriate to this combination is — 1 degree of lunar motion to one year of time. The Moon lacks 9 degrees 48 minutes of perfect conjunction with Jupiter, which equates to 9.8 years — somewhat unrealistic and hardly likely to lift the depression of the querent.

There is yet another way. The Moon is co-ruler of the querent, Mars is significator of the quesited, and the Moon applies to a sextile of Mars by 21 minutes of arc. The Moon is fixed and succeedent, which equals one degree per year, so 21 minutes of arc = 4.2 months, and so I judged.

In the first part of November the same year (exact date not recorded), the querent was offered and accepted a newly built council flat; about 4.5 months — pretty good timing!

Figure 18: Will Meg be found?
Meg was a delightful Border Collie pup recently acquired by a near neighbour of mine. One Sunday I was passing my neighbour's house when I saw her in a most distressed state. She told me that on the previous day she had taken a friend's baby for a walk in its pram in another part of town. Meg went too, without a lead. Suddenly she missed the dog; it had completely disappeared. A thorough search of the area revealed no trace of the animal, and the local police and RSPCA had been contacted to no avail. Whilst walking home it occurred to me to ask the question.

The Ascendant of the chart is just over 27 degrees, but I had not recorded the exact time the question occurred to me so I decided to treat the chart as radical. As the querent I am shown by Mercury. A neighbour is of the third house, so her significator is Mars. The Sixth House has dominion over small pets, so to find the significator of Meg we must count six houses from the third (my neighbour's pet). This brings us to the eighth house of the chart, so the dog is ruled by Mars too.

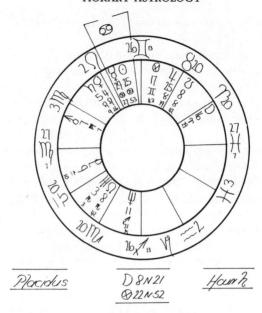

Placidus   ☽ 8N21   *Hour ♄*
               ☉ 22N52

Figure 18.
Will Meg be found?
18 July 1976 10AM0 GMT 51N46 0W28

The condition of Mars should reflect the state of both dog and owner. Consider the owner. She is distressed and confused: Mars is square Neptune. The acuteness of her distress may be deduced from Mars in Virgo (the natural sign of health). Consider the dog. She is lost and confused: Mars square Neptune. I did not fear for the dog because, apart from the Neptunian influence, Mars is not afflicted. Indeed she is protected by a good aspect to the Nodes. It also seemed that the dog was running free. The nature of Mars combined with Neptune in Sagittarius suggested it, and there was no indication of restriction or confinement. How will the matter end?

We know that the fourth house of the chart has dominion over the End of the Matter enquired about. The End of the Matter as far as I, the querent am concerned, is shown by the fourth house of this chart. However, my neighbour's fourth is the fourth from the third, and the dog's fourth is the fourth from the eighth. Jupiter rules my fourth and my neighbour's fourth; the Sun rules the dog's fourth. Jupiter is unafflicted; he applies by trine to the Ascendant and is in close sextile with the Sun, which also applies well to the Ascendant. Thus I concluded that the matter would end happily for all concerned.

To discover what will happen next in any matter, look to the first aspect of the Moon. Here she applies closely to a sextile of Fortuna. That is what will happen next: success — the dog will be found.

The Moon applies to the Sun by square aspect and that is her final aspect. A square can bring matters to perfection when the planets apply from angles, particularly when they are dignified. The Lights are angular; the Moon occupies the sign of the Sun's exaltation while the Sun occupies the sign of the Moon. I take this as a mutual reception, and it is a favourable indication which may promise the assistance of a third party.

My final judgement was that the dog would be found, and soon. I did not give this judgement to my neighbour, as I had erected the chart for my own interest and my neighbour was unaware of my celestial pursuit. See how ineffective I am in the chart; Mercury combust and mute.

The next day my neighbour contacted schools in the area where the dog was last seen and arranged for the loss to be announced at their assemblies. At about 4 p.m. the dog was found by three school children. It is interesting that the mutual reception involved the Sun and Moon; Sun, ruler of the End of the Matter for the dog; Moon, children.

The Moon is just 1 ¼ degrees from an exact sextile with Fortuna; Meg was found 1 ¼ days from the time of the question. The Moon is angular/cardinal representing 1 degree per day in the Generally Accepted Measure of Time.

Direction by House or Sign
To discover in which direction any lost person, animal, or thing is, refer to Figure 19. Whenever you find the significator by house or sign, it is in that direction you must look to find what is lost. In Figure 19, Mars (significator of the dog) is near the twelfth cusp, which corresponds by house to east-south-east, and the animal was found three miles away east-south-east.

Distance
The calculation of distance is a tricky business, but there are two

(a) Direction by house

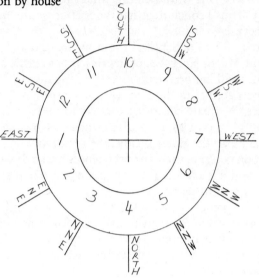

(b) Direction by sign

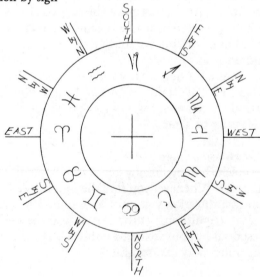

Figure 19.

methods of finding distance which I will reproduce here. The first according to Dr W. J. Simmonite (*Horary Astrology: The Key to Scientific Prediction*). First calculate the latitude of the significator of the thing lost, and then refer to the following table:

Significator	Without latitude	North latitude	South latitude
Angular	Nearby	Some furlongs	Some miles
Succeedent	Some furlongs	Some miles	Some leagues
Cadent	Some miles	Some leagues	Some degrees

If you wish to know the number of miles or degrees of distance, take the number of degrees between the significator of the querent and the significator of the thing lost in the chart, or the number of degrees before a major aspect occurs between the significators. Then according to the sign occupied by the significator of that which is lost, calculate as follows:

Significator in a *cardinal* sign — every degree = 2 miles
Significator in a *mutable* sign — every degree = ½ mile
Significator in a *fixed* sign   — every degree = ¼ mile

Ivy Goldstein-Jacobson (*Simplified Horary Astrology*) suggests the following method. First take the significator of that which is lost and apply it to the following table:

Significator	Without latitude	North latitude	South latitude
Angular	Nearby	1 mile	2 miles
Succeedent	½ mile	2 miles	3 miles
Cadent	1 mile	3 miles	indefinite

These basic distances must then be multiplied by the number of degrees separating the Moon and the significator of that which is lost. When a significator is in cadent houses and southern latitude, it is most probably too far away to judge distance accurately.

In Figure 18, Mars, significator of the dog, held north latitude and occurred in a cadent house. According to Simmonite this would suggest that the dog was some leagues away, which was not the case. Since both dog and owner are signified by Mars, it is not possible to apply the next formula. However, it is true to say that Mars held only 1 degree of north latitude, so if treated as having no latitude the first reading would be that the dog was some miles distant.

According to Ivy Goldstein-Jacobson's method, the significator

(Mars), cadent with north latitude equals three miles, which would be fine if one did not have to multiply three miles by the number of degrees separating the Moon and Mars.

Obviously it is unfair to judge any method from a single example, and since the question itself did not actually ask about direction or distance, it is unreasonable to demand such information from the chart. So bear these tables in mind, and test when the opportunity arises. I shall deal further with location later, in Chapter 15, 'Loss and Theft'.

At the beginning of this chapter, I gave the formula known as the Generally Accepted Measure of Time, which uses the Moon as the principal timing agent. It can also apply to the faster moving planets, Mercury and Venus. A further indication of timing may be obtained from planets, when significators, perfecting an aspect by *normal motion*. If Mercury and Mars be significators, and apply to each other by, say, sextile aspect, and that actual aspect perfects in three days, it may well be that the thing demanded will occur in three days. One really has to bear all these possibilities in mind, examine the chart, see what is available and come to a judgement through a mixture of common sense and inspiration.

So far I have attempted to acquaint you with a foundation for horary astrology upon which you may build with your own experience. You should now know how to approach a chart, what basic considerations to apply, and how to recognize conditions which traditionally assist or deny perfection.

The remainder of this book consists of a collection of detailed judgements of some of the most interesting charts that have come my way. These are my own judgements, so they naturally reflect my own approach to horary astrology. I offer them to you as a guide, as examples of horary astrology in action. I have arranged my examples into seven groups: Marriage and Relationships; Births and Babies; Property; Education; Career and Status; Loss and Theft; Sickness and Death.

I have deliberately avoided taking you through each horary house in turn and setting down a collection of rules appropriate to the judgement of questions of that house. This has been done often enough before, and I have mentioned elsewhere in this work details of the few publications I have found valuable. In any case I do not work that way. One needs to be aware of the basic conditions that deny or assist perfection, and one needs to take great care over the appointment of significators. The rest of it is up to you.

Each horary chart is a unique experience, whatever the question. As long as the chart is radical, the astrologer is entitled to expect that the chart will reflect the condition of the querent or person enquired about, and the circumstances surrounding the question. Every radical chart has a message to give. If the astrologer has a good knowledge of his craft, he should be able to interpret that message. So when you have a radical chart, consider the question and study the chart. Allow your consciousness to open. The chart will either speak to you or it will not. If it does, you have a basis for judgement; if it does not, you should put it aside.

PART TWO:
COLLECTED JUDGEMENTS

10.
MARRIAGE AND RELATIONSHIPS

It is probable that more questions and problems are put to the astrologer under this heading than any other. We are living through a revolution in personal relationships. We must be very careful indeed when approaching questions of this nature. It is most important that our advice should not help to break up a marriage and deprive children of a parent. Naturally the astrologer cannot undo what has already been done; nor is it for him to moralize. But all relationships pass through periods of stress and difficulty, frequently returning to a happy state once the crisis has passed. It is wise to proceed with caution.

Generally speaking, most relationships fall under the dominion of one of three houses. The seventh house rules marriage partners and permanent relationships; the fifth house rules lovers and 'illicit liaisons'; and the eleventh house has to do with friendships of the platonic kind. When selecting the significator of the other party in a question about a relationship, one should be careful to get it right. There may often be some confusion as to whether the other party should be shown by the seventh house or by the fifth — as a permanent partner or a lover. It will be necessary to enquire into the nature of the relationship and then to make a judgement about the significator based upon the particular circumstances, and also to take advice from the chart itself, for it is often most helpful.

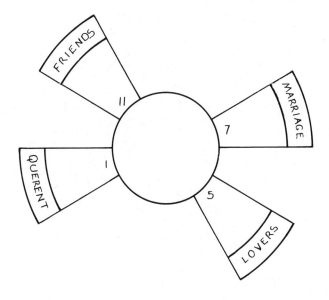

Figure 20. Marriage and relationships.

Figure 21: Will I get married this year?
I once had a job which required me to sit at a desk in the reception hall of a large company and check visitors in and out. There were often long periods when I had no visitors to attend to at all. But an astrologer always has something to do, and I made use of the time by working on various astrological projects. My interests were well known in the building. One afternoon, while I was working on my charts, a young executive type approached me and said: 'What about my horoscope then?' I had promised to look at his nativity some time before. I told him that it would be a few weeks before I had anything worthwhile to give him. Then, in a tense and slightly embarrassed way, he blurted out — 'I want to know if I'm going to get married this year.' Ah, thought I, a horary question. I noted the time and promised an answer after the weekend.

The chart is radical, and apart from the fact that it can be read,

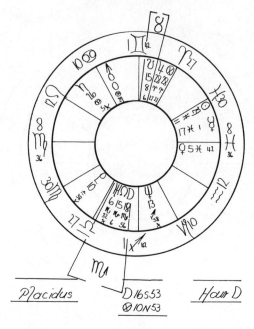

Figure 21. Will I get married this year? 19 March 1976 4PM9 GMT
London

the Moon of the horary chart is conjunct the Descendant of the
nativity. An excellent confirmation of the validity and nature of the
question.

The question is directly concerned with the possibility of marriage,
so it is clearly a seventh house question. The significators are: Mercury
as lord of the Ascendant (the significator of the querent), and Jupiter
as lord of the seventh house (the significator of the quesited). We
must not forget that the Moon is co-significator of the querent, and
that Venus by her nature has general dominion over relationships.

Will marriage take place this year? If marriage is to take place
within the year, the chart must indicate it. We would expect either
the querent's significator, Mercury, to be approaching an aspect with
the significator of the quesited, Jupiter, or the Moon to be
approaching an aspect with Jupiter. There are no such indications,
so the first impression is that marriage will not take place this year.

Now, there is an aspect between Mercury (querent), and the joint-ruler of the seventh house, Neptune. However, it is a square aspect, and Mercury (the faster planet) is separating from Neptune (the slower planet). Separating aspects do not indicate future happenings and a square aspect rarely symbolizes that a thing will be achieved. In this case though, the Mercury-Neptune contact well describes past events: the querent had experienced much confusion and disappointment in relationships, and he had been engaged three times.

The Moon, co-ruler of the querent, is in trine aspect to seventh house Mercury, but again this is a separating aspect. Note that the Moon is aspecting from the third house (questions), and Mercury — the natural ruler of questions, and significator of the querent — is in the seventh house of marriage. Has he proposed marriage? Has he enquired (third house) whether a girl will marry him (seventh house)? It certainly looks like it.

Let's leave Mercury where he is for the moment, sitting in the house of marriage, weak in the sign of Pisces. Let's give our main attention to the Moon as co-ruler of the querent. The Moon is just leaving a trine of Mercury (the querent has proposed marriage), and is going to a trine of Saturn in the eleventh, and then to a trine of the Sun at the eighth cusp. It would be difficult in this chart to see the Moon-Saturn contact as indicative of marriage, but it would not be at all difficult to see the Sun-Moon trine as symbolizing matrimony. In the first place the Sun and Moon may be seen as representing male and female coming together; secondly, a good applying aspect between the lights is, of itself, a powerful indication of success.

The querent asks whether marriage will take place within the year. So how long would it take the Moon to complete her promised trine with the Sun? The Moon is fixed and cadent, and according to the Generally Accepted Measure of Time (see Chapter 9), this represents an indeterminable period. Therefore there is no likelihood of the Moon linking with the Sun in the forseeable future, and certainly not within the year.

The End of the Matter (fourth house), is ruled by Jupiter, which although conjunct the Part of Fortune, is also square Saturn, and this must surely be a delaying influence. Furthermore, the confusing and worrying Neptune is in the fourth house squaring Mercury in the seventh. There are clear indications that marriage will not take

place, but a couple of other influences seem to remove all vestige
of doubt. The Moon is besieged (between two malefics). She is
therefore contained and cannot act without stirring up evil vibrations.
This condition, more often than not, denies perfection. The Moon
is also upon the degree of Serpentis, the most evil degree in the
zodiac, and I have never known anything prosper when this degree
is prominent in a horary chart.

So the main significator of the querent, Mercury, is weak in Pisces
in the house of marriage; the Moon, co-significator of the querent
is besieged in the third house upon the degree of the horrible
Serpentis. The querent is trapped. He is under duress and distressed.
If what has happened until now has led to his entrapment, then
it must be his proposal of marriage. He has proposed marriage and
he is trapped, but there is no indication that marriage will take place.

Mutual reception can often provide a way out of a situation. Here,
the Moon and Mars are in mutual reception, so the Moon (querent)
has an escape route if it is desired. The Moon can exchange signs
with Mars (although both planets retain their original degrees). If
this option is taken, the Moon moves to the eleventh house, where
she applies to a conjunction of Saturn, and Mars moves to the third
house where he applies to a conjunction of Uranus. Thus may the
Moon be removed from the evil clutches of Serpentis. Mutual
reception often argues the assistance of a third party.

My judgement at the time was: Marriage will not take place this
year; I cannot calculate from this chart when marriage will take place;
if the querent is deeply concerned and distressed by the matter, he
should cease to worry because it might well be resolved through the
assistance of a third party. The querent will remain single for the
foreseeable future.

When I gave my judgement to the querent he received it without
comment. Over a month later he said to me: 'You were right.' He
would not elaborate, but he is a Sun-Cancer and the Water signs
are notoriously secretive. It eventually emerged that the querent had
proposed marriage but subsequently got 'cold feet'. The girl
concerned approached the querent's best friend and discussed it
with him, and in the end she decided not to accept his proposal.

It is very interesting that the influence of the friend was symbolized
by the mutual reception, and that the Moon — aside from being
co-ruler of the querent — is also lady of the eleventh house of friends.

Figure 22: Are Judy and I suited?
Peter and Paula were married. They were both social workers. Judy was also a social worker. In fact she had been Paula's superior, but she had lately left social work to take up the study of law with the aim of becoming a solicitor. Peter and Judy began an affair unbeknown to Paula (Peter's wife) or Fred (Judy's husband). Peter's wife (Paula) found out, left the marital home and went to America.

At the time the question was asked, Peter was living alone, his affair with Judy was continuing, and Fred was still blissfully ignorant. The question was not asked of me directly but was passed to me for judgement by another astrologer.

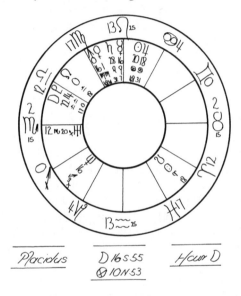

Figure 22. Are Judy and I suited? 13 July 1978 1PM40 GMT London

The first consideration is that the chart is not radical, less than 3 degrees of Scorpio rise, and the Ascendant is located within the *via combusta*. The message to the astrologer is that, at the time the question was posed, events had not moved far enough for judgement to be given; the question is premature. At this point the matter could have been concluded. I could have said, 'It is too early to say,' and left it at that. However, I had a chart, and I like to investigate any chart, radical or not, if only to see *why* judgement cannot be given, but whatever conclusions I come to, I would not normally give judgement to the querent on a premature chart. In this case I was able to give judgement to the other astrologer purely for the pleasure of the exercise.

Peter is ruled by Mars. He is the querent and shown by the Ascendant. Judy is signified by Jupiter, ruler of Peter's fifth house, for she is his lover. Mercury represents Judy's husband, Fred, because he is shown by the seventh house from the fifth (the husband of Peter's lover) or the eleventh house of the chart. Paula, Peter's wife, is shown by Venus, lady of the seventh house.

Now Mars (Peter) is exactly square to Neptune (joint-ruler of the fifth), and this contact certainly describes Peter's situation. He is involved in an illicit love affair (square = illicit; Neptune = secret). Peter is also in a state of Neptune-inspired confusion, and his position in Virgo suggests feelings of guilt. It may well be that the affair began about six months before when the Moon was sextile Neptune (by the Generally Accepted Measure of Time). There is a favourable contact between confused-guilty-mutable Mars, and the extremely powerful Jupiter, so Judy is considerably more powerful than Peter in this matter.

Judy (Jupiter) is in the ninth house, strong by house and sign; the Moon has lately squared Jupiter from Libra (the natural marriage sign), thus provoking the negative side of Jupiter — recklessness and adventurism. It is most interesting to find that, given Judy's legal ambitions, her significator — legal Jupiter, is exalted in the ninth legal house. This suggests that her ambition for a legal career takes precedence over all other considerations as far as she is concerned. Peter appears to be the servant of Judy (Virgo), be he only responsible for sexual service (Mars).

Now Fred (Judy's husband) is shown by Mercury. He must be a major consideration because he is conjunct the Midheaven and exactly trine Neptune. Given his prominence in the chart, I thought it unlikely that he would remain in ignorance of the affair for long.

Peter's wife Paula (Venus), had lately moved from a conjunction with Saturn in Leo into Virgo. She has embarked upon a new course, and although she applies to Peter (Mars) by conjunction, the perfection of the aspect is denied by refranation, so it does not seem likely that they will get together again.

My judgement to the other astrologer was: The chart does not permit us to give a judgement to the querent. He is in a most confused and guilty state and is not capable of making any reasonable decision about his situation at this time. Judy is going for her legal career come what may, and at the moment she is using Peter. Fred is about to figure in the matter and until he has added his weight no judgement can be made. The Moon is in the twelfth house; she applies to none of the significators; all her aspects are in the past. From Peter's point of view the matter cannot end well.

Shortly afterwards Fred found out about the affair by discovering a letter (Mercury) that had passed between the lovers. He was not a little put out, his Leo pride having been ruffled, so he gave his wife a beating. This brought matters to a head, and although Judy showed some interest in continuing the affair, Peter lost interest thinking it a waste of time.

Peter's wife Paula came back across the Atlantic planning to return to America permanently. She insisted that their jointly owned flat be sold. Not being able to afford to buy another place, Peter was obliged to find rented accommodation. He lost his wife and his flat. Things did not end well for the querent.

Figure 23: *Will we get married?*

This question was asked by another astrologer. Some time after it was posed I met him for the first time. He then asked me to look at the chart and perhaps give a judgement. At the time my judgement was a cautious yes. Three years later I discovered that my judgement had been wrong: the couple did not get married and the relationship came to an end. I include this example to show just how careful one must be in the allocation of significators, and to warn against the temptation of trying to wish or will a certain outcome against basic considerations. The astrologer is no magician; he is an interpreter. It is important that we analyse our failures, for that is how we learn.

First of all I will repeat here the detailed judgement I sent to the querent:

The chart has Leo rising so you, the querent, are signified by the Sun (and the Moon as co-ruler of every question). This is a question about marriage and is therefore a seventh house matter. Thus the significator of the quesited is Saturn. It may also be valid to consider your intended as a subject of the fifth house if this house is descriptive of your present relationship.

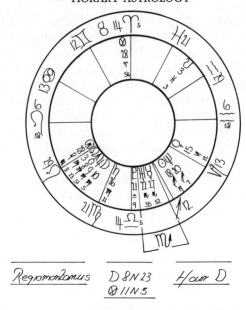

Figure 23.   Will we get married? 10 December 1979 8PM01 GMT
Dublin

Consider the main significators — the Sun and Saturn. The Sun
applies to Saturn by square aspect. This does not encourage optimism
initially. However, the Sun is dignified in its own house, and because
you and your girlfriend behold each other by square there is clearly
some difficulty between you. With your significator being strong
in its own house in the optimistic sign of Sagittarius, it is clear that
you are stronger for the marriage than the other. She is symbolized
by Saturn in Virgo, so her attitude will be cautious and much
concerned with some kind of status matter.

I have found that where the Moon applies well to the Sun, and
that application is not interrupted by an intervening malefic, a matter
usually (nay, always in my experience) ends well. Now in this chart
the Moon applies to the Sun but the aspect is a square. However,
the Moon applies from the house of her exaltation to the Sun in
his own house. Thus are both Lights dignified. So we have an
intriguing situation and one which it is not easy to judge. The
indicators are finely balanced.

So I have to make a judgement: yea or nay. My judgement must be yea. The Moon is closely conjunct Jupiter, and although this is strictly a separating aspect it is so close to the Moon to allow a translation of light to Venus, and the first aspect the Moon makes is a trine with well-aspected Venus. Venus rules the End of the Matter as far as you are concerned, so this argues a happy ending for you.

The most important aspect of all is the Moon's applying conjunction with Saturn, for if we allow the Moon to act as your co-ruler, we see that you and your girlfriend will eventually conjoin. In a case like this where Saturn is a main significator, we do not read him as a malefic.

I am intrigued by Mars. We can see him as a significator of your girlfriend (fifth house); Mars is applying to a conjunction with Jupiter (the legal planet) and in this chart the ruler of the ninth legal house. We could say that your girlfriend is close to a legal ceremony. Mars is also ruler of the tenth house, which is the End of the Matter as far as your partner is concerned.

I am conscious that this is a difficult judgement and risky, but on balance I must say yes. By the Generally Accepted Measure of Time the exact conjunction between the Moon and Saturn occurs within sixteen months.

I think my first error in this judgement was to give the girlfriend partly to Saturn. The question is about marriage. Saturn is the significator of marriage in this chart, but Jupiter is the significator of the girlfriend as ruler of the fifth house of the chart. The promise of marriage as far as the querent is concerned would be shown by a favourable aspect between his significator — the Sun, and the significator of marriage — Saturn. The Sun does not apply to Saturn by favourable aspect, but by difficult square. If Jupiter is the significator of the girlfriend, the significator of marriage as far as she is concerned is Mercury, ruler of the seventh from the fifth. There is no contact between Jupiter and Mercury.

I made much of the applying aspect between Sun and Moon, the aspect is a Square, but I sought to mitigate that negative influence by saying that the Moon had dignity because she occupied the second house (the natural house of Taurus in which sign the Moon is exalted), and that the Sun had dignity because he occupied the fifth house (the natural house of Leo in which sign the Sun has dignity). I read this relationship as a kind of mutual reception. Such reasoning is perhaps bold — it goes beyond tradition and there is no precedent for dignity by house alone. This does not mean that it is necessarily invalid, but it is not wise to allow a judgement to rest upon it.

The pattern of Jupiter-Moon-Venus is a perfect example of translation of light. Venus is separating from a trine of Jupiter, but the Moon is separating from Jupiter and applying to Venus. She is therefore bringing the light of Jupiter back to Venus: she is translating light. Considering that Venus is ruler of the fourth house (End of the Matter), and the natural ruler of relationships, it is not wrong to see this translation as indicative of marriage, and this pattern is really the only positive suggestion that marriage might occur. Yet I should have recognized that Venus going to a square of Pluto in Libra in the fourth house could well destroy the marriage prospects.

Finally I made the mistake of calling Mars significator of the girlfriend. This was just plain carelessness and indefensible. Also, the close conjunction between the Sun (querent) and Neptune in the fifth should have set my alarm-bells ringing. Neptune is the planet of delusion, infatuation, worry, etc., and by its close contact was obviously shedding its confusing ray over the querent. While I could defend the judgement upon the basis of translation of light, against it we have the Moon applying to a square of the Sun, the Sun applying to a square of Saturn, and the Sun conjunct Neptune. On balance the judgement should have been No!

When I originally judged this chart I did not include the Part of Marriage. I have entered it here and it is interesting that it is in the seventh house of the girlfriend, the eleventh of the chart, and that house is ruled by Mercury which squares the Part of Marriage. Whether this is important is open to debate, but it is just one more little indication against marriage.

By such disasters as this do we poor astrologers learn our trade through bitter experience.

Figure 24: Will I get divorced?

The lady querent in this case had visited a number of mediums, Tarot readers and the like, and all had told her that she would be widowed. Her marriage was under some strain; her husband had serious financial problems and was drinking heavily. She was considering divorce, but could not reconcile this with the messages she had received, so she posed the question.

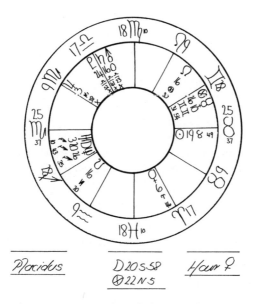

Placidus   D 20 S 58   Hour ♀
            ⊕ 22 N 5

Figure 24. Will I get divorced? 10 May 1982 9PM03 GMT E. London

Mars is the primary significator of the querent. He is weak in Libra and retrograde. The poor state of Mars in the sign of Marriage testifies to the poor state of the marriage. The Moon, co-ruler of the querent, is not in good condition either; she is besieged on one side by Uranus and on the other by Neptune. The significator of her husband is Venus. She is also weak by sign and stands opposed to his wife. The degree upon the cusp of the seventh is 26 Taurus, or Caput Algol, which is not a helpful indication. It all looks most strenuous until one realizes that the principal significators, Mars and Venus, are in mutual reception.

When the lady asked the question her significator was retrograde, but three days later Mars turned direct. It is as if she had been seeking a way of escaping from her marriage (moving towards Virgo out of Libra), but she stops at the very edge and then begins to go back into the marriage again. This would tend to suggest that very soon after she posed the question, she changes her mind and moves into the marriage again. Although Venus and Mars are opposed, the aspect cannot be seen as strenuous to the relationship because of the reception between them. On the other hand, Mars (querent) will by direct motion begin to close with the first house Uranus, that could indicate divorce, but in view of the condition of the Moon, the querent will not find it easy to move in the matter. She is certainly confused and uncertain (Neptune).

The key to the question is probably the reception between Venus and Mars, and it may be seen in several different ways:

(1) By exchanging positions with Venus, the querent could move herself from an unsatisfactory marriage, but she would move to the first degree of Aries, and that would seem to symbolize a completely new life, so we could say that the reception symbolizes a divorce.

(2) If she removes herself from her marriage, her husband's significator goes to the tenth house, where he becomes strong in Libra, and this raises the consideration of how much the querent herself is responsible for the weak state of her husband.

(3) The reception can also symbolize the querent lending herself and her strength to her husband in a time of crisis.

The querent appears to have a choice. She can divorce if she likes, but I do not think she will.

Her husband is in the middle of a serious financial crisis, the ruler of his money is Mercury (lord of the eighth house of the chart). Mercury is strong in Gemini, but he has to pass through an aspect with Saturn, Pluto and Neptune. There is a difficult path to tread, but he will eventually close with Fortuna.

My judgement was that there would be no divorce, that the querent would begin to take a positive attitude towards her marriage which would be saved by the reception. Eighteen months later no divorce had occurred and the crisis which provoked the question seemed to have passed.

Figure 25: (1) Will my relationship with my wife continue to be a lasting and fulfilling one? (2) Will I make an ongoing success of my career in films, and when will I make my first feature film?

This is a very interesting chart for two reasons. Firstly it demonstrates how to handle a question asked by letter from a location in southern latitude; and secondly it shows how a heavy mundane conjunction symbolized a personal situation.

I first met the querent in London when he attended some of my astrology classes. He was working as a film producer. He was really learning his craft and was ambitious to rise to the top of his profession. An Australian and an Aquarian, a lovely man; we became friends. He married a charming and beautiful English girl and they seemed very happy. Eventually he returned to Australia to pursue his career there.

One day I received a letter in which he posed the above questions. At that stage he was just uneasy about his marriage relationship. Things were not as they should be, and he sensed that problems might arise.

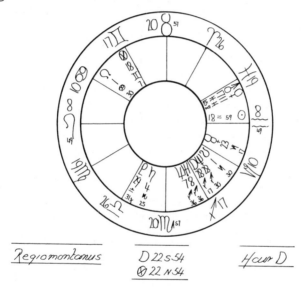

Figure 25. (1) Will my relationship with my wife continue to be a lasting and fulfilling one? (2) Will I make an ongoing success of my career in films, and when will I make my first feature film? 8 February 1983 8AM4 GMT 27S15 152E5

Now, when the astrologer receives a question by letter, it is necessary to erect a chart for the moment he reads the question, and to locate it for the place the letter was written from. In this case I read the question on 8 February 1983 at 8.04 a.m. GMT, and the letter was written from latitude 27 degrees, 15 minutes south, and

longtitude 152 degrees, 5 minutes east. The astrologer can be forgiven
for fearing, as he erects his chart for the other side of the world,
that the result will bear no relation at all to the matter enquired
about. My eyebrows raised slightly when I discovered that the horary
chart's Ascendant was within 8 minutes of arc of the position of
the querent's radical Pluto (joint ruler of his natal seventh house)
and that the horary Midheaven was within 24 minutes of arc of his
wife's natal Moon. There were other contacts also, but within a few
degrees.

The primary significators are: the Sun for the querent, Saturn
for his wife, Venus for his career, and Jupiter (lord of the fifth) for
his creative endeavours. The Moon, of course, is co-significator of
the querent.

I did not regard the second question as being of much importance.
I am acquainted with the querent's nativity and his progressions,
and there is no doubt in my mind that he will be highly successful
in his chosen career. In the horary chart, Venus, lady of the tenth,
is exalted. His creative ability (fifth house) is clearly shown by the
Moon conjunct Neptune (films) close to the benefic fixed star
Regulus. Jupiter, ruler of the fifth, is strong in Sagittarius, closely
applying to Uranus (photography and technical ability). The querent
was just looking for reassurance. I gave my main consideration to
the first question.

The querent (the Sun) is in the seventh house. He is in good aspect
with Fortuna but has no aspect to anything else. So he is in the house
of his wife, in her power, because that is where he chooses to be,
and because that is his dearest wish (Fortuna — eleventh house).
He is a Sun-Aquarian and needs his marriage relationship to be a
friendship; that is the nature of Aquarius. There he sits, fixed and
solid, in the house of his marriage, and he does not want to go
anywhere else.

What about his wife? She is shown by Saturn, in Scorpio, in the
third house of the chart, and about to turn retrograde. She is in
the querent's house of communication, he is finding it difficult to
communicate with her, and since she disposes of him (Saturn disposes
of the Sun), he feels ineffective. Why is his wife in this condition?
She is in the querent's third house but in her own ninth house. She
is in a foreign place, in a fixed sign, and about to turn retrograde.
Could it be that the excitement and stimulation of actually moving

to the other side of the world is passing? Venus, lady of her fourth and ninth houses, has passed a trine with Saturn. Saturn in Scorpio invokes feelings of depression. Could she be suffering from depression and turning in upon herself? She is a Sun-Sagittarius, with Sagittarius rising and the Sun conjunct Jupiter, yet in this chart she is symbolized by Saturn about to turn retrograde, and this symbolism is completely at odds with a free and expansive nature.

It seemed to me that the chart was saying: 'Here is a Sagittarian bridled, and if the restricting bridle cannot be shaken off, frustration, lethargy and depression will be the result.'

In order to see what is likely to happen to the wife, to see in which direction she will move, we must see what Saturn will do: retrograde, change sign and move towards a conjunction with Pluto in Libra. An ominous indication indeed for the fortunes of the marriage — a Saturn-Pluto conjunction in Libra, the sign of marriage. Now, considering that the querent had expressed unease about his marriage, this coming aspect looked rather drastic. However that is the direction in which his wife was clearly going. So the future of the marriage was bound up with the heavy Saturn-Pluto mundane conjunction.

From the simple diagram of the Saturn-Pluto conjunction, Figure 26, it will be seen that at the time the question was asked on 8 February 1983, the exact conjunction had already taken place. However, Saturn would turn retrograde at 4 Scorpio and begin moving back towards a conjunction with Pluto again; but he would not quite make it. During the summer months of 1983 he would come very close, within 1 degree, but would then begin to separate again. From this pattern we might be justified in thinking that the marriage would come very close to breaking up, but that the querent's wife would stop just short of taking an irrevocable step.

It was clear that there would be a crisis which would probably reach its height in the summer of 1983. My next move was to see if there was a way out of the situation for the wife. An escape route could be provided by a mutual reception, but there is no reception for Saturn in the chart, so she was bound for a Plutonian experience come what may.

I told the querent that there was likely to be a Plutonian experience, and that it would probably mean a temporary separation. I could not give a definite Yes to his first question because his wife

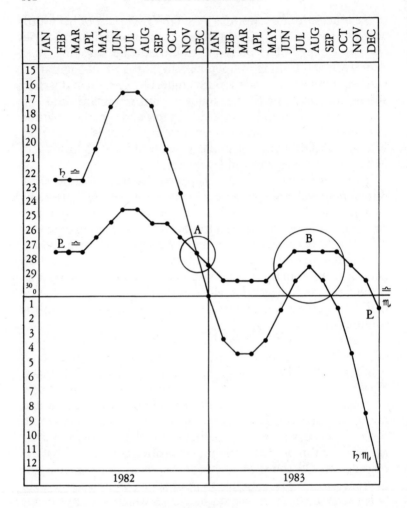

A = Exact ♄ ☌ ♇
8 Nov 1982 1AM51

B = Summer 1983

Figure 26.   Diagram of Saturn-Pluto conjunction relating to Figure 25.

had to go through her transforming experience, but by the time Saturn came back into Scorpio, things may well have resolved themselves. I thought that the summer crisis could be best handled by his wife returning to England during that time, but this did not happen.

In the early summer of 1983 the querent came to London for a few days and we met. He and his wife had separated at this time. She had become involved with someone else. But despite his deep distress and anger, I formed the impression that all he really wanted was for his wife to come back to him again. In late October 1983, I was delighted to receive a letter telling me that his wife had come home and they were attempting to make their relationship work. He had remained constant in his desire for the survival of his marriage, his significator in Aquarius in the seventh house without aspect. They are delightful people, they deserve each other, and I hope they make it. It will be noticed that Moon and Fortuna are parallel in this chart, and this is another indication of a successful outcome.

11.
BIRTHS AND BABIES

Pregnancy and related matter come mainly under the dominion of the fifth house. Questions of this category come in infinite variety. Some ask if they are pregnant — hoping that they are, others make the same query — praying they are not. Boyfriends ask if their girlfriends are pregnant, and some if they are the true father of the child. Others just want to know if they will ever have a baby.

The following framework through which the astrologer may determine whether a woman is pregnant was laid down by William Lilly.

Indications of Pregnancy

The lord of the Ascendant or the Moon in aspect to the ruler of the fifth house, or a benefic in the fifth house; in mutual reception or involved in a translation of light; and free from affliction.

A dignified Moon in mutual reception with any planet at an angle.

The lord of the Ascendant or fifth house in good aspect with, or in mutual reception with any angular planet.

The lord of the Ascendant in good aspect with the cusp of the Ascendant from a good house.

The Moon in the seventh house in good aspect with the lord of the seventh in the eleventh; or the Moon in the eleventh in good aspect with the lord of the eleventh in the seventh.

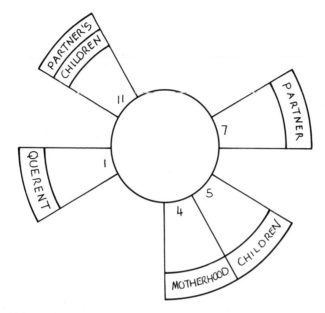

Significator of babies and motherhood: ☽
Natural sign of motherhood: ♋ Natural sign of children: ♌

Figure 27.

The Moon in the tenth house applying to the lord of the Ascendant or lord of the fifth house by good aspect, or by bad aspect with mutual reception.

Jupiter in the first, fifth, seventh or eleventh house unaspected by Saturn or Mars, with those malefics slow in motion or retrograde.

A fixed sign upon the Ascendant with a benefic in the first house, or the lord of the fifth strong in the first or tenth.

If none of the above conditions are present, or if barren signs are on the Ascendant or fifth cusps; or if malefic planets are in the first or fifth houses, or afflicting the rulers of the first and fifth and the Moon, the lady is not pregnant.

Fruitful signs are: Cancer, Scorpio and Pisces.

Barren signs are: Gemini, Leo and Virgo.

Length of Pregnancy

To determine how long a subject has been pregnant, isolate the rulers of the Ascendant and the fifth house, and the Moon; note what separating aspects occur between them. If one of the significators is separating from another by:

Conjunction — She has been pregnant for — 1 month
Sextile   — She has been pregnant for — 2 or 6 months
Trine   — She has been pregnant for — 3 or 5 months
Square   — She has been pregnant for — 4 months
Opposition — She has been pregnant for — 7 months

Viability of the Child

Traditional signs that the child will not survive infancy are: the lord of the fifth house or the lord of the Ascendant, retrograde, combust, or cadent; or weak by sign and afflicted by the ruler of the eighth or twelfth; or weak by sign and afflicted by malefics in the eighth or twelfth; there being no mitigating influences.

Lilly also states that if the fifth house is occupied by Mars, Saturn or the South Node, the child will not survive; and Ivy Goldstein-Jacobson maintains that malefics in the fifth or eighth, afflicted by a planet in the fifth concerns the possibility of the child's survival. She considers that where Neptune is involved there is the possibility of abortion or miscarriage; with Uranus, Caesarean section; with Mars, haemorrhage; with Saturn, malformation; and when the Moon and Mars are in aspect, a surgical operation of some kind is necessary. She further states that where the lord of the fifth is in mutual reception; or framed (that is, between) Venus and Jupiter; or if Venus and Jupiter are angular in the chart, the child will survive. The Sun in the fifth house, while not necessarily denying conception and the production of a child, does not traditionally favour the child's survival.

Twins

The double-bodied signs are: Gemini, Sagittarius and Pisces. When double-bodied signs appear upon the cusp of the Ascendant or the fifth house, with a benefic in that house, and the Sun and Moon and ruler of the first and fifth occupy double signs, there is a strong possibility of twins. Another indication of twins is when the Moon,

Venus and Jupiter are all in double-bodied signs.

Sex of the Child

Only when the question is specifically asked should a judgement be attempted. Then, consider the rulers of the Ascendant and the fifth house, the cusps of those houses, and the Moon; the more of these that occupy masculine signs, the more likely the child is to be male, and vice versa for female.

It is now appropriate to examine three charts, all for the straight question, 'Am I pregnant?' In each case, while pregnancy would have been rather inconvenient, it would not necessarily have been unwelcome.

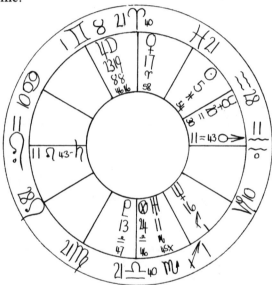

Figure 28.
24 February 1977 3PM3 GMT London

Figure 28: Am I pregnant?
The indication of pregnancy here is the Moon in the tenth house applying to Jupiter (lord of the fifth) by conjunction in Taurus. However, the perfection of that conjunction is interrupted by the Moon squaring Mercury before closing with Jupiter. It is unnecessary to speculate about the meaning of the Moon-Mercury square, because

with Saturn at the Ascendant retrograde the question is destroyed. This is a primary consideration, and the answer to the question is a firm No. The querent was not pregnant.

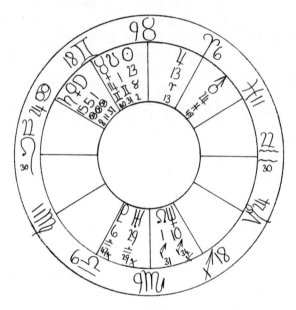

Figure 29.
14 May 1975 11AM0 GMT London

Figure 29: Am I pregnant?
The Sun is lord of the Ascendant and Jupiter lord of the fifth house. They are not in aspect. The Moon in the eleventh house in Cancer applies to a conjunction of Venus. This combination has a strong flavour of motherhood about it. However, the ruler of the fifth is in Aries closely applying to a square of Saturn. There might have been a great wish to have a baby (eleventh house), but despite the strong Cancer influence Saturn prevailed; the lady was not pregnant.

Figure 30: Am I pregnant?
Venus is lady of the Ascendant and Saturn lord of the fifth house. They are not in aspect and Saturn is retrograde in the barren sign of Leo. The Moon is strong in Taurus but not only is she Void of Course, but close to the degree of the malefic fixed star the Pleiades

Figure 30.
12 January 1976 11PM13 GMT London

(the Weeping Sisters). The lady is not pregnant; with a Void of Course Moon nothing will come of the matter; and so it proved.

Figure 31: If I come off the Pill will I become pregnant?
In this case the lady asked the question because she had no desire to become pregnant. I include this example because it is one of the best and clearest demonstrations of a mutual reception that I have.

The querent is ruled by Venus, and Venus is in Gemini (not a fruitful sign). She is also combust, moving into the rays of the Sun; since Venus is lady of the eighth house (Sex), I thought it well described the condition of the querent when she asked the question — barren.

It is the mutual reception that is the key to the resolution of this question. Mutual reception implies a choice, so if she has the mind to do it, Venus may exchange signs with Mercury, and move from the 13th degree of Gemini to the 13th degree of Taurus. Therefore, if the querent chooses to abandon her barren state (as she may —

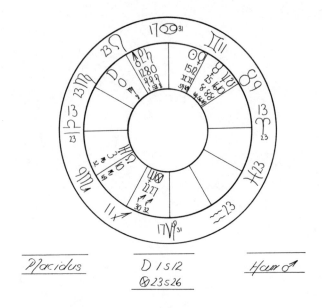

Placidus   *D 1 s 12*   *Hour ♂*
                    ⊗ 23 s 26

Figure 31.
If I come off the Pill will I become pregnant?
8 June 1976 2PM8 GMT London

the matter is in her own hands), she becomes extremely fertile,
because Venus becomes dignified in earthy Taurus and applies to
a conjunction of Jupiter in the eighth house of sexual power.

My judgement was that the likelihood of pregnancy was very high
if the querent came off the Pill.

Figure 32: Will my sister-in-law be safely delivered?
The querent in this case was very worried about the condition of
his sister-in-law, and it was a chart which required a delicate
judgement. His sister-in-law was pregnant and she was having a
difficult time. She had lost her first child some years before — it
had not survived more than a few weeks. She then produced a healthy
son. She was advised against having any more children, but she and
her husband desperately wanted a daughter before considering their
family complete.

We have a third-party question, since the querent is asking about
the affairs of another. Where in this chart do we find his sister-in-

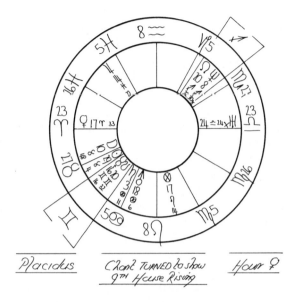

Figure 32.
Will my sister-in-law be safely delivered?
20 May 1974 12PM07 BST 51N25 2W25

law? The querent's brother is shown by the third house of brethren, so the house of his wife must be the seventh from the third, so we count seven cusps from the third and arrive at the ninth of the chart. For convenience I have turned the chart to show the ninth house rising, so the querent's sister-in-law is now at the ascendant. Her significator is Mars, which occupies Cancer, and she is a Sun-Cancer. What state is she in?

She is in trine aspect to a powerful Jupiter, but since Mars moves faster than Jupiter, the aspect is separating and the influence is passing. She applies by square to an angular Uranus, and that worried me. Venus also applies to Mars by square and I didn't like that either. So there she is, weak in Cancer (Mars has his fall in Cancer), applying to an angular malefic by square, and being applied to by a weak Venus, also by square. It seemed to confirm her condition; she was weak and there was concern for the success of the pregnancy.

The unborn child is signified by Mercury, lord of the fifth house, and although Mercury is strong in Gemini I did not look with optimism at the conjunction with the South Node. However, I was intrigued by the position of Mercury — intercepted in the second house, contained within the body of the sister-in-law, her most precious possession at that moment.

The condition of the Sun really gave me cause for concern, for it was upon the Pleiades, the malefic fixed star degree known as the 'Weeping Sisters'. This promises tears, so my first impressions were not optimistic, and I feared for both mother and baby.

Then I thought more about the Moon. She is very powerful, exalted in Taurus in the first house and applying well to Mars. A strong and fruitful Moon bringing assistance to the weak Mars. Then I noticed it: a translation of light! The Moon translates light between Jupiter and Mars. Translation is a very useful thing. It can bring the 'thing demanded' to perfection, but as I have mentioned there are two concepts of translation of light.

The first, set out by Lilly, and therefore given preference by the purists is as follows. When two significators have been in aspect, but that aspect has already perfected so that the faster of the two planets is moving away from the slower; but then another planet, faster in motion than both of them, separates from an aspect of the slower planet and applies to an aspect of the faster planet, then the third planet is reuniting the original — it is translating light from the slower back to the faster.

The second concept, put forward by Ivy Goldstein-Jacobson, says that where you have the same condition, a separating aspect between two significators, and a third and faster planet aspects each of them in turn, then you have translation. You will see that in this case we have a translation of the second variety.

So who was I to take notice of, Lilly or Goldstein-Jacobson? What a dilemma! Actually there was no dilemma at all, I seized upon it at once; as far as I am concerned they are both right. To have ignored such mitigation in a delicate chart on the grounds that it was not sanctioned by Lilly would have been negative. It was there in the chart to be read. In the end I made judgement as follows:

Mars is weak and described the condition of the sister-in-law. Mars is afflicted by Uranus from the house of the querent's brother and by Venus his ruler. Yet, the Moon is angular. She is exalted and fruitful and lending her strength to Mars. Furthermore she is bringing the power of a dignified Jupiter back to the assistance of Mars by a translation of light.

Thus I considered that the sister-in-law's dearest wish — to produce a healthy daughter — would be granted by the magic of Jupiter from the house of hopes and wishes. The child, shown by Mercury, is strong in Gemini and applies to Fortuna in the fourth by close sextile, thus giving protection from the influence of the South Node.

Although the Sun is upon the malefic 29 Taurus, it is isolated and the Moon cannot perfect a conjunction with it before a change of sign (a New Moon is traditionally highly malefic in horary astrology).

I concluded that the matter would end well, and it did — three-and-a-half months later a healthy daughter was born. By the Generally Accepted Measure of Time, the event approximated to the Moon perfecting her sextile with Jupiter, so the wish was granted. Despite my judgement, I breathed a sign of relief when I heard that mother and child were doing well.

Let me return for a moment to the Sun. As lord of the fourth he does rule the End of the Matter. Sitting as he does upon the degree of the 'Weeping Sisters', he promises tears, and the late degree suggests the end of something. The End of the Matter was that there could be no more children: the family was complete.

Now if the first house of the turned chart is the house of the querent's sister-in-law, the seventh house is the house of his brother. He has Uranus upon his cusp and Venus (his ruler) is applying by opposition to Uranus, this rather suggests that the brother's condition is about to undergo a dramatic change.

Coming back again to the Sun, it occurs in the second house of the chart, which is the brother's eighth house of sexual power. Shortly after the birth of his daughter, the querent's brother had a vasectomy, and according to his graphic account of the operation (he is a Sun-Scorpio with a gift for telling a tale), it certainly brought tears to his eyes.

My original judgement ended with my considering the matter would end satisfactorily and that the sister-in-law's dearest wish should be granted. The matter of the vasectomy did not form part of that judgement. Although I am being wise after the event, I would suggest that the chart does describe what happened. It is amazing how much information can be squeezed from a horary chart.

Figure 33: Will I have a baby this year?

This question was posed by a young married lady, and it is one of the handful of truly remarkable horary charts that has come my way. It is a fifth house question, and so Mercury is ruler of both querent and quesited. In such cases, as I have explained, we allow the Moon to become primary significator of the querent, and Mercury to retain rulership of the quesited. On the face of it, this is a simple straightforward question. What has the chart to say about it?

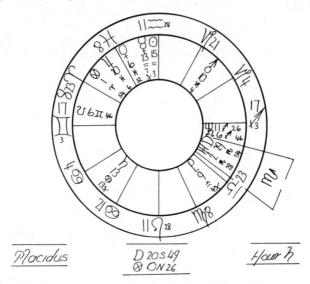

Figure 33.
Will I have a baby this year?
4 February 1975 Noon GMT 51N33 0W06

The first thing it says is that the Moon is Void of Course. She can make no aspect with any other body before she leaves the sign she occupies: she is within only 6 minutes of arc of a change of sign. The normal interpretation is that nothing will happen: the Moon is applying to nothing, so nothing may be expected from the matter enquired about.

Mercury is retrograde and combust, and therefore weak and ineffective. Despite the fact that the Moon has been allowed to assume dominion over the querent, I would still look to Mercury for a description of her condition. With Mercury retrograding back to a combust relationship with the Sun in Aquarius (a sign not noted for its fertile nature), the querent is weak, ineffective and infertile: not very promising. More often than not, a retrograde Mercury tells the astrologer that he is not in possession of all the facts concerning the matter. The querent is either keeping something back, or something else must come to light before the matter can be properly judged.

With the Moon Void of Course, and Mercury retrograde and combust, the surface answer to the question is a simple No. The querent will not have a baby this year. The chart gives no indication of it.

From the manner in which the question was put, it was clear that the querent very much wanted to have a baby, and I thought that if she wanted a baby so much, it naturally followed that she must have been doing something practical about getting one. So without even referring back to the querent I had two subsidiary questions: Why won't she have a baby this year? When will she have a baby?

I thought it very likely that I had not been told all there was to know about the matter, for Mercury was retrograde, the Moon was in secretive, mute Scorpio, and the querent is a Sun-Pisces. At first I was tempted to give the answer No, and leave it at that. But when the girl posed the question, I was moved strongly because it was obviously a matter of deep concern to her. I just could not accept a plain No. I had to delve deeper into the chart.

Several factors provoked serious thought. There was a heavy emphasis on the sixth house; the Moon and Uranus were intercepted there in Scorpio; Neptune and the North Node were there in Sagittarius. Venus ruled the sixth house and she was exalted in Pisces close to the eleventh cusp. She separated from a trine of Uranus and applied to a square of Neptune. It seemed that there might be some kind of medical problem and it came to my mind that she should seek advice.

Then I was much interested in the Mars-Saturn opposition across the second and eighth houses; masculine Mars is powerful in the sign of Capricorn, and he occupied the eighth (sex) house, while Saturn is weak in Cancer (the sign of motherhood) but he occupied a critical cardinal degree. While I was pondering upon this opposition a picture formed itself in my mind. I saw the powerful masculine symbol in the shape of exalted Mars, trying to force penetration of the female organism symbolized by Cancer, but meeting obstruction from Saturn so that the seed could not settle and germinate. I saw the second house as representing the organism of the querent, her most intimate and precious possession. I thought I had got to the heart of the problem: an obstruction in the body of the querent to the seed of her husband.

The problem seemed surmountable because Jupiter and Venus trined Saturn. Furthermore Jupiter occupied the eleventh house and was dignified in Pisces and exalted Venus was applying to a conjunction of Jupiter. The dearest wish of the querent was to have a baby. Surely with all this going on in the eleventh house there must be a strong chance that her wish would be granted — eventually.

So, I judged that the answer to the question was No, the querent would not have a baby this year, but she should be encouraged to seek medical advice because some kind of adjustment appeared necessary to remove a block to fruitfulness. Since the block was symbolized by Saturn, and Saturn occupied a critical cardinal degree, I thought the matter would reach culmination point in just under three weeks. (Mars applied to an exact opposition of Saturn by about three degrees, and Saturn was retrograding back to perfect the aspect thereby hastening matters.) My opinion that the matter was about to culminate was reinforced by the fact that the Moon was about to change sign into free-ranging Sagittarius.

I told the querent that I didn't think she had told me the whole story (which she strongly denied); that the answer to the question was No; and that she should seek medical advice because there seemed to be some kind of obstruction, but one which was not serious. After some adjustment she should be able to conceive, and the matter would be settled in about three weeks.

At the time I made this judgement I was breaking new ground. I had never before read great detail into a chart with a Moon Void of Course and a first house ruler retrograde and combust. I considered I was taking a risk, but I gave the judgement because I felt I must. To my utter astonishment the querent understood the judgement perfectly. She revealed that she had been using the Coil, that she had consulted a doctor about having it removed and that the operation would take place within ten days. As it happened it took place within a week, and seven days later she asked me a further question, shown in Figure 34: Now when will I have a baby?

I set to with confidence and drew up the chart — only to find the question premature; the second degree of Cancer at the Ascendant — it was too early to say. I was baffled.

Mercury was still retrograde and the Moon was again Void of Course. The rising sign and the prominence of the Moon at the Midheaven both emphasized the nature of the question — motherhood, but apparently not yet. I was obliged to tell the querent that it was too early to give a judgement, and although I was confident that she would eventually have a child (Venus was closer to Jupiter, lord of the eleventh, than it was in the first chart), I could not say when.

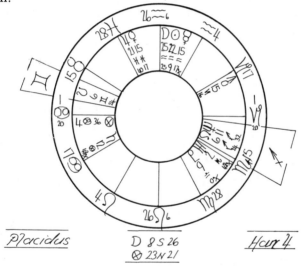

Figure 34.
Now when will I have a baby?
11 February 1975 12PM30 GMT 51N33 0W06

Actually I was concerned by the chart. The New Moon was close to the Midheaven, and as I have said a New Moon in horary astrology is traditionally a most malefic indication. For some reason the situation in respect of a pregnancy would have been too much for her to handle. Furthermore, Mercury, lord of the fifth, was retrograde. There was more to come before a baby, but the long-term promise remained. You will notice two slight but striking differences between this chart and the first one. First, Mars is now *separating* from an opposition of Saturn instead of *applying to it*, symbolizing the removal of the obstruction. Secondly, Venus is now only 6 degrees short of a conjunction with Jupiter, lord of the eleventh house, whereas in the first chart the distance between them was 14 degrees: the granting of her dearest wish was getting closer.

Needless to say, the querent was not pleased with my judgement. She asked no further question about the matter. She didn't need to: very soon she was pregnant. However, the child miscarried, and shortly after that she moved and I did not see her again. I subsequently learned from a mutual friend that she produced a healthy son in June 1976, fourteen months after the first question; and you will recall that Venus was 14 degrees short of Jupiter in the first chart.

I found this case a truly remarkable demonstration of the power and literalness of horary astrology. It did more to persuade me to become a horary disciple than any other. The first chart reflected the physical obstruction in the most amazing way; the second chart showed the removal of that obstruction, but also warned that the matter was premature, and that there was something else to be experienced. But both charts showed that the querent's wish to become a mother would be granted eventually.

Figure 35: Is she pregnant?
This question was asked by a girlfriend of the subject without her knowledge. The querent is always shown by the Ascendant, and since the question concerns a friend, the subject is shown by the eleventh house. The chart has therefore been turned to put the eleventh house on the Ascendant.

The significator of the subject is the Moon. This is a fifth house question, so the significator of the quesited (pregnancy) is Mars, lord of the subject's fifth house. It is interesting that the Moon falls in Leo, the natural fifth sign.

Traditionally the barren signs are Gemini, Leo and Virgo. You will see that Mars, ruler of the fifth, is in Virgo; the Moon, lady of the first, is in Leo; and if you apply this chart to the rules given at the beginning of the chapter for the determination of pregnancy, the answer to the question must be No.

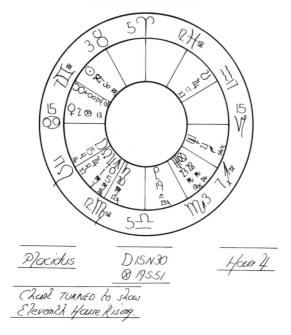

Placidus   D 15N30   Hour 4
             ⊗ 19S51

Chart TURNED to show
Eleventh House Rising.

Figure 35.
Is she pregnant?
20 May 1980 0PM30 GMT London

It is a mistake to follow blindly sets of rules laid down by others (with the possible exception of considerations before judgement). I have never understood, for example, why Virgo should be designated as a barren sign. It is earthy and associated with harvest. It probably has something to do with the symbolism of the Virgin Mary and the immaculate conception, and it is true that the glyph for the sign seems to indicate female legs firmly crossed. However, it is not good enough just to apply the chart to the traditional rules and then dismiss or accept the question on that basis. We must see what the chart has to say.

First of all, Cancer, the sign of motherhood is at the first house. Venus is in Cancer. She is not ruler of the fifth or first, but she is in the sign of motherhood. Now Venus is in close aspect with the Mars-Jupiter conjunction, and Mars is lord of the fifth. Venus separates from Jupiter and applies to Mars, and this has the appearance of a translation of light. The fact that Venus had made a sextile aspect with Jupiter encouraged me to think that the subject was pregnant. It seemed to me that Venus in Cancer sextile Jupiter in Virgo symbolized conception — the planting of the seed. Now there are those who say Mars is a destroyer of life, particularly when he is in a barren sign. Yet he also represents the masculine principle, and it would not be difficult to see the conjunction of Mars and Jupiter in Virgo as the planting of seed also. That conjunction actually took place in the first degree of Virgo.

Although Venus appears to be translating light between Jupiter and Mars, and promises to make a sextile aspect with Mars, that promise is not fulfilled because Venus is about to turn retrograde. She in fact turns retrograde on 26 May at 2 degrees 33 minutes of Cancer, then moving back to sextile Jupiter again. Figure 36 shows the pattern.

Now let's use our common sense. We have been asked about pregnancy. The good aspect of the two benefics occurring some time before the question, with one of those benefics in Cancer, suggests conception to me. A further sextile occurring some time after the question suggests birth to me, and that is the way I read it. The baby is Venus in Cancer. Is there a better astrological description of a baby than Venus in the early degrees of Cancer? In any case she is lady of the eleventh house of hopes and wishes and lady of the fourth house (End of the Matter).

The main worry I faced with this chart ws the degree of the Sun upon the malefic fixed star the Pleiades (Weeping Sisters). However, the Sun may be removed from that degree by a reception with the Moon. The Moon may move to strength in 16 Taurus and the Sun may move to the degree of the benefic fixed star Regulus at 30 Leo. So I judged the woman to be pregnant — and so she was. At the time of the question she was about three months pregnant.

This chart does not conform to the table for discovering the length of time a woman has been pregnant as set out at the beginning of this chapter. The subject produced a healthy child on 17 November 1980.

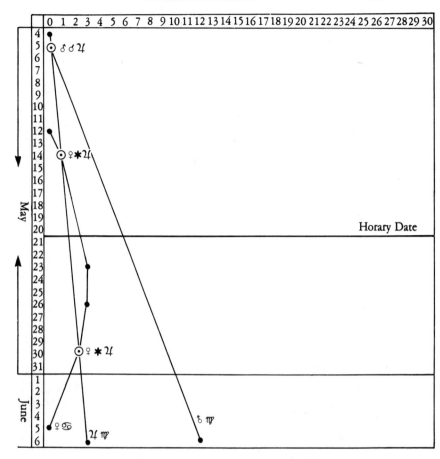

Figure 36. Diagram of aspect relating to Figure 35.

12.
PROPERTY

In questions concerning property, the first house and its ruler signify the querent, whether buyer or seller; the seventh house signifies the other party, whether buyer or seller; the fourth house, its ruler and the moon represent the property under consideration; and the tenth house and its ruler are concerned with the price of the property.

Traditionally, the fourth house and its ruler, and any planets in that house, denote the condition and description of the property. The Element of the sign upon the cusp of the fourth may also be seen to show the kind of land upon which the property stands (if such information is appropriate to the question). Generally, Fire signs show hilly or mountainous land; Earth signs indicate level ground and good soil; Air signs represent undulating land; and Water signs show low-lying land with water on it or nearby. If the quality of the land is an important consideration, a more detailed description may be drawn from the chart by considering the quality and condition of the ruler of the fourth and planets in the fourth. For example, if an afflicted Saturn is in the fourth in a Fire sign, it may be said that the land is dry and stony, while a good Jupiter in an Earth sign in the fourth would show good and fertile land. Further, the old astrologers would have looked to the tenth house to show the plentifulness or otherwise of trees and wood, and to the seventh house for other plants.

If a question is concerned with a specific transaction (Will Mr X buy my house?), the astrologer should look to the ruler of the first (seller) and the ruler of the seventh (buyer), and see if there is any

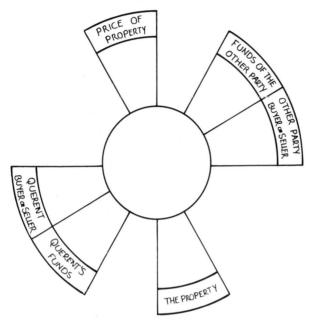

Universal co-significator of property: ☽
Natural sign of property: ♋

Figure 37.   Property

promise of agreement between them. If they apply by conjunction
or good aspect, or they are in mutual reception, there is a strong
promise of a deal being struck, and the transaction will be amiable.
A square aspect between the significators can also allow a deal to
be closed, but it will be a hard bargain and not easily completed,
unless there is a reception between them. If the significators oppose
each other, the matter may be completed, but the querent is likely
to regret it.

The Moon separating from a malefic and applying to a benefic
is to the advantage of the buyer, but when she separates from a
benefic and applies to a malefic, it is to the seller's advantage. Where
there is translation of light or collection of light, the translator or
collector often represents an agent or middleman of some kind who
acts to bring the significators of buyer and seller to agreement.

Questions concerning the buying or selling of property usually involve a financial consideration, so the rulers of the second houses of those involved in the transaction, as well as the condition of the houses themselves, are important. The second house of the querent is obvious. The second house of the other party is the second from the seventh (the eighth of the chart). From an examination of these houses and their rulers, the astrologer is able to see who is most likely to do best from the deal. The better the condition of the lord of the tenth, the more expensive the property is likely to be.

If there is a malefic in the seventh and he is not the lord of the seventh, great care should be taken with the legal agreements drawn up between the parties.

If there are malefics badly aspected in the tenth, or the tenth house is afflicted, there is unlikely to be a sale or purchase. To see how the matter will end, consider the fourth house. If there are fortunate planets in the fourth, if the lord of the fourth is in the fourth, or the house is well aspected, the matter will end well to the satisfaction of both parties to the transaction.

Figure 38: Will we sell our house for a good price?

The querent was about to leave the country and move overseas. He had put his house on the market and was anxious to know whether he would obtain a good price for it.

Venus is the significator of the querent (seller), Mars is for the buyer, and the Moon signifies the house for sale. The price is shown by Saturn, lord of the tenth.

The first consideration is whether there is any relationship between the rulers of the first and seventh, and there is; Venus applies to Mars by square aspect. We may deduce from this that there could well be a sale, but it will be a hard bargain, and since the ruler of the seventh is stronger than the ruler of the first, it is the buyer who has the advantage. The Moon, significator of the house, is upon the cusp of the buyer's second house (the eighth of the chart), and it may be that the buyer is doubtful if he can raise the necessary money to purchase the house. The nature of Sagittarius, however, suggests that he will stretch himself to the utmost in order to achieve it, for he very much wants to possess it.

The significator of the price is Saturn, and he is in Virgo and not that strong in the figure, so the price is reasonable. Venus in the fourth suggests that it is a pretty house and nicely decorated, and that it is of good value.

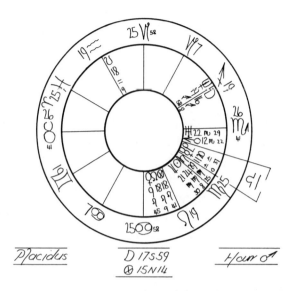

Figure 38. Will we sell our house for a good price? 16 September 1980
9PM7 Wandsworth

With Venus, the North Node and Fortuna all in the fourth house, and an aspect about to mature between Venus and Mars, the suggestion is that there will be a sale. One might look askance at the Moon's applying conjunction with Neptune, and square with the Sun and Jupiter, but before she can perfect her aspects with these planets, she makes a trine with Fortuna in the fourth, so the matter ends successfully to the satisfaction of both, and so it did.

The greater strength of the significator of the buyer in the chart, together with the square between him and Venus, reflects the situation of the seller. He was going abroad and had to sell his house, and although he was reasonably satisfied with the outcome, his options were rather limited, for time was not on his side.

Figure 39: Will we get Hunter's Lodge?
The querent was anxious to obtain a certain property, 'Hunter's Lodge', and she posed the above question.

The significator of the querent is Mercury; the seller is shown by Jupiter, lord of the seventh; the property is also signified by Jupiter,

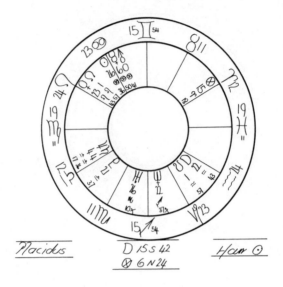

Figure 39.   Will we get 'Hunter's Lodge'? 19 July 1981 9AM10 GMT
E. London

and the Moon may also be seen as a significator of the property.
Since Sagittarius appears upon the fourth cusp, the name 'Hunter's
Lodge' seemed almost appropriate.

The querent (Mercury) is separating from Hunter's Lodge, which
is not very promising — and it has nothing else of importance to
do in this chart. The Moon has no contact with the querent or Jupiter;
all she can do is oppose Venus, and her final aspect is a square with
Uranus. Notwithstanding the presence of Neptune in the fourth
where he is well aspected, my judgement was that the querent would
not get Hunter's Lodge, for the ruler of the fourth was conjunct
to the powerful Saturn in the first house. And so it turned out.

Figure 40: Will it all go through? When will it be sorted out?
The querent was trying to buy a flat, but matters had come to a
standstill because there were problems with the mortgage. She was
beginning to despair of the whole matter, and she posed the
question.

Although this question is concerned with property to some extent,

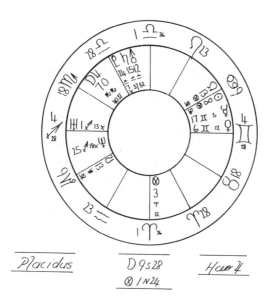

Figure 40. Will it all go through? When will it be sorted out? 30 June 1982
6PM2 GMT London

its main purpose is to discover whether the mortgage the querent requires will be forthcoming, for that is the only thing which is holding up completion of the sale. Our main concern must therefore be concentrated upon mortgages, and this is an eighth house matter (other people's money).

The significator of the querent is Jupiter, the significator of the mortgage is the Moon, but the Sun must also be counted as a significator by virtue of his position at the cusp of the eighth house. The Sun (mortgage), separates from a good aspect of Jupiter (querent), but the Moon is separating from a conjunction of Jupiter and applying to a trine of the Sun. Therefore, although at first sight the mortgage appears to be running away from the querent, the Moon is reuniting the Sun and Jupiter by translation of light, so there is a strong indication that the querent will get the money.

The question also asked *when* the matter would be resolved. The Moon is fixed and succeedent, and by the Generally Accepted Measure of Time, a degree of lunar motion equates with a year. With the Moon applying to the Sun by just over a degree of arc, the traditional timing would be just over a year. This is unrealistic, so I judged the matter would be settled in just over a month, and that indeed proved to be the case.

The question asked specifically about the mortgage and the time of completion. This was the mandate given to the astrologer. If the question had also asked about the condition of the flat, etc., I would have shuddered at the applying Mars-Saturn conjunction in the tenth house of the chart. Mars is signifier of the flat through his rulership of the fourth house, and Saturn rules the querent's second house. Mars is weak in Libra and Saturn is exalted; it is just about as nasty a combination as you can get, and it is even worse by virtue of the fact that the Sun applies to that conjunction by square aspect. I did not take account of this pattern at the time of judgement because I was only concerned with the mortgage, but as it turned out it presaged serious difficulties for the querent.

After the sale was completed, she soon discovered that there was a serious problem with dampness, and no amount of investigation could locate its source. One theory was that the flat was built over an underground stream. The problem was so bad that the querent began proceedings against the freeholder in an effort to get the sale revoked. The freeholder actually made an offer to repurchase the property but when he learned that it had been condemned by the local authority he withdrew the offer.

Now, just over two years after the sale, the querent has a flat in which she cannot live, the dampness problem has not been solved, and legal proceedings continue. The whole business has cost her a great deal of money so far, and even if her legal fight ends successfully, she will be very lucky indeed if she does not end up substantially out of pocket.

I have always maintained that the astrologer should stick closely to his mandate when giving judgement to a querent, but examples such as this make one wonder.

Figure 41: Will I get the house?

The querent lived in a council house with her husband and daughter. It was a two-bedroomed house and adequate for their needs. However, the querent's husband suffered badly from asthma, and it became important that he should have a bedroom of his own. The problem became critical and the querent set her mind to

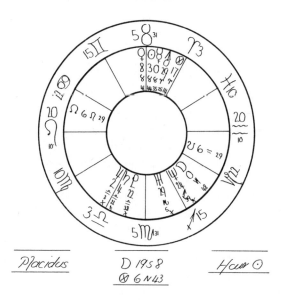

Figure 41. Will I get the house? 24 April 1981 12PM05 GMT
51N46 0W28

resolving it. One day she was walking in another area of the town
in which she lived, when she saw an empty council house which
suited her needs admirably. Now, she really liked the house and
was convinced that the house liked her. So with the determination
typical of a Scorpio she decided that she was going to have it.
Enquiries at the Housing Department met with a blank refusal,
despite the fact that her application was backed up with powerful
medical evidence.

There were reasons why it would have pleased the officials at the
Housing Department to refuse the application, but I am not able
to disclose them. However, it became necessary for the querent's
husband to make a personal appeal to the chairman of the relevant
committee, and it was when that appeal had been made and the
outcome was awaited that the question was posed.

A house, being astrologically a fourth house matter, is ruled by
Mars; the querent is ruled by the Sun. Mars is strong in his own
sign and about to change from Aries into Taurus, and I thought
the imminent change very significant. But there is no contact between

Mars and the Sun. However, the Moon (a significator of the council house), applies to the Sun by trine aspect, so it could be said that the house is coming to the querent. There is a square with Jupiter for the Moon to handle before she perfects her trine with the Sun, but I would not count this impedition as one powerful enough to deny a successful outcome, because Jupiter is benefic by nature. What is more discouraging is that the Moon also applies to a square of Saturn, and Saturn is powerfully placed in Libra. So I had to consider a very tight pattern, the Moon applying to a square of Jupiter, a trine of the Sun, and a square of Saturn, all within a space of 4 degrees.

As I have said many times, I regard a good aspect between the Lights as a very strong sign of a successful outcome for the querent. The fact that the perfection of the aspect between the Lights was interrupted by a difficult aspect to Jupiter did not prevent me from accepting the promise of success indicated by Sun and Moon, but I would never judge success with the Moon going to a hard aspect of Saturn. Nonetheless in this case the Moon perfected her aspect with the Sun just before she squared Saturn, so I judged that the querent would get the house. I saw the Sun at the Midheaven as symbolizing the chairman of the committee to whom the querent's husband had appealed, and I saw him interposing his influence to prevent denial.

I called at the home of the querent to give her my judgement, but before I could say anything she told me that she had been offered the house and had accepted. Apparently the house had first been offered to another person with a more deserving medical problem, but that person had refused the offer because of the poor decorative state of the property. It had then been offered to the querent. The prior offer is shown very nicely by the retrograde Jupiter in Libra. The Moon had to surmount that hurdle before joining with the querent, and I like the reason for the refusal: poor decorative state — Jupiter retrograde in Libra.

This example demonstrates vividly that a good aspect between the Lights is, of itself, a powerful indication of success, no matter what comes afterwards. One could say that with the perfection of the aspect between Sun and Moon, the matter ended. It is not necessary to go beyond it. Here is a case for the astrologer sticking strictly to his mandate, as opposed to the last example where going a little further would have produced more valuable information.

The seventh house of this chart rules the astrologer, and he is shown by Saturn retrograde in Aquarius. I was actually prevented from delivering a judgement to the querent, and I have found this occurs quite often when the ruler of the seventh is retrograde.

Whether to Stay in a Certain Place or Move

Questions often raise the issue, in one way or another, of whether a certain move would be beneficial to the querent or not. Logic would prompt the astrologer to reason that if the significators of the querent are applying to good planets, then what is in the future will be beneficial; but if his significators apply to evil planets, what is to come is unfortunate. However, if a querent asks whether he should stay where he is or move somewhere else, who is to say whether the good or evil indications apply to his remaining or his removal? In the judgement of such questions the following rules will be of assistance.

Arguments for staying

Consider the rulers of the Ascendant, the fourth house and the seventh house. If the ruler of the fourth is not a malefic and is in the seventh, and the rulers of the first and seventh are not malefics or have dignity, and if all these significators are direct in motion and have aspects with benefic planets, do not move.

If the Moon separates from an aspect of a benefic, or if a benefic planet is in the first house, do not move.

Arguments for moving

If the lord of the seventh is in aspect with a benefic and the lord of the fourth is in aspect with a malefic, it is better to move.

If the ruler of the first separates from a bad aspect of the ruler of the sixth, eighth or twelfth, and the Moon separates from a bad aspect of a malefic (when that malefic is ruler of the fourth or seventh and not the significator of the querent), then move.

If a malefic is in the first or fourth and retrograde, it is an argument for removal.

13.
EDUCATION

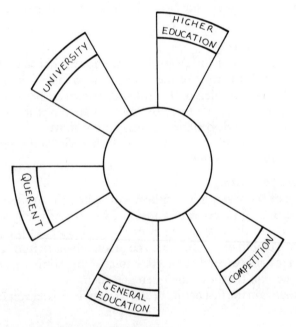

Universal co-significators of education: ☿ ♃
Natural signs of education: ♓ ♐

Figure 42. Education.

Questions concerning education often crop up, mainly from anxious parents who have not been given their first choice of secondary school for their child, and also from worried students hoping to get to university. Questions of this kind fall mainly under the third and ninth houses — the third for primary education and the ninth for higher education. Secondary education may come under the third or the ninth — one must be guided by the chart. There is some dispute over what house has control of universities. Some say the ninth, but I am inclined to give consideration to the eleventh as well. With any question which has to do with the passing of examinations, it is also wise to take note of the fifth house, because this house is usually important where any kind of competitive element is involved. Obviously, Mercury and Jupiter have a special influence in educational matters.

Figure 43: Will my daughter go to the school of her choice
This question came from an anxious mother who had just learned that her daughter had not been offered a place at the secondary school of her choice. The child had taken the news badly and her mother was about to appeal against the decision.

The Moon occupies the fifth house of children, confirming the true interest of the querent (her child's welfare). Because of her position the Moon may also be taken as a significator of the daughter. The mother is shown by Venus, lady of the Ascendant, and the daughter must also be ruled by Jupiter, lord of the fifth. The daughter's house of education is either Mars, ruler of her third (the seventh of the chart) or Venus, ruler of her ninth (the first of the chart).

Jupiter (daughter) has no contact with Mars or Venus, but the Moon does apply to Venus by square aspect, and interestingly Venus is in Gemini (third sign) in the ninth house of the chart. It seems clear that the chart is pointing to Venus as the significator of the school, so the key aspect in this case is the Moon square Venus. Matters may be brought to perfection through square, but it is usually exceedingly difficult, and it would be better if the two significators involved were strong, which they are not, although the Moon is disposed of by Venus. The Moon is besieged by two malefics (Mars and Neptune); and Jupiter (the daughter) in the twelfth house of the chart and retrograde is without power. The Ascendant (mother) is in the *via combusta* and conjunct Pluto. The querent also seems

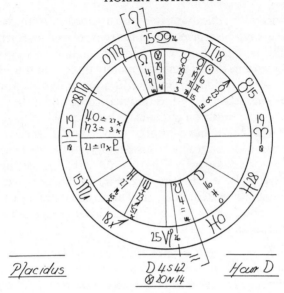

Placidus   ☽ 4s42   Haur ☽
              ⊗ 20N14

Figure 43.
Will my daughter go to the school of her choice?
27 May 1981 3PM31 GMT 51N46 0W28

to be without power and obsessional about the matter, and she was. I was not encouraged by this chart. The only mitigation seemed to be that Venus trined the Ascendant, and that the final aspect of the Moon was a trine with Fortuna at the Midheaven.

On balance I would not give an outright No to the querent, but I said things did not look hopeful, and I awaited developments. The mother's appeal was turned down by the educational authorities. This for most parents would have been the end of the matter, but when an angry mother has the Sun in Scorpio and a Mars-Saturn conjunction on the Ascendant, she needs little prompting to go into battle. Her husband had been involved in local affairs and he knew the channels. The mother was inclined to take the matter further by securing an interview with the top education official in the county, and she asked a further question, shown in Figure 44: Is the matter worth pursuing?

In this chart Saturn is conjunct the Ascendant, yet it is in the twelfth house and the Ascendant is separating from it. However, Saturn is lord of the fifth here and therefore the significator of the

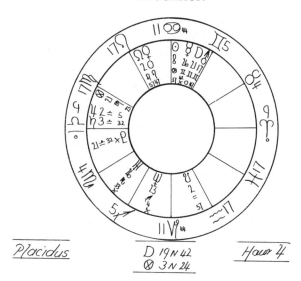

Figure 44.
Is the matter worth pursuing?
30 June 1981 12PM19 GMT 51N46 0W28

querent's daughter. Venus is still ruler of the school, and she is now in Leo, applying well to the daughter (Saturn), and there is no impediment to the sextile aspect perfecting.

Mercury is retrograde in the ninth and the Moon will soon make a conjunction with him, but she does have to pass an opposition with Neptune first. This does suggest worry and confusion, but I was much happier with this chart than the former one. My reading of the significance of Mercury was: a change of mind on the part of the education authorities (ninth house). I thought this chart looked good, and my only reservation was rising Saturn, for at worst he destroys a question in this position, and at the very best he considerably reduces the degree of success. In this case, however, he was a main significator and Jupiter was about to conjunct him. I judged the matter might well end successfully, with Venus (mother and school) applying at once to Jupiter, and with Jupiter then going on to benefit Saturn (daughter and End of the Matter). So I said: 'Yes, the matter is worth pursuing.' The querents did pursue it, and her daughter ended up going to the school of her choice.

Figure 45: Will I pass my examinations and go to university?
A male student had taken his examinations and was awaiting the
results. He was quite agitated and posed the above question.

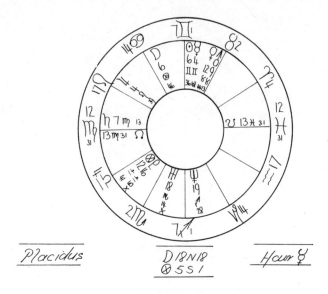

Placidus   D 18N18   *Hour* ☿
                 ⊕ 5S1

Figure 45.
Will I pass my examinations and go to university?
28 May 1979 12PM45 GMT 51N46 0W28

At the time, this question aroused a good deal of interest among
some of my astrological friends. Before we even look at the
significators, two factors stand out in the chart. First, Saturn is
conjunct the Ascendant within 5 degrees. Saturn conjunct the
Ascendant or in the first house of any horary chart by tradition
destroys or damages the question. It is one of the main considerations before judgement. Secondly, Mercury, ruler of the querent,
is combust. According to Lilly, this condition suggests that 'Neither
the matter propounded will take or the Querent be regulated.' In
other words, the matter will not be successful.

Despite these two restrictions I decided to judge the chart. I
reasoned that perhaps the influence of Saturn was far enough away
from the Ascendant (which was separating from Saturn) to

considerably reduce its maleficity; and I saw the Sun as the father of the querent, and his father was leaning very heavily upon him at the time to do well and gain a place at a university. The combust condition of Mercury also testified to the lack of confidence the querent was suffering from. He did not really think he had much of a chance, so the question was asked in pessimistic spirit.

For the purposes of this particular exercise I ignored Mercury, and took my main reading from the Moon as co-ruler of the querent. The Moon was strong in Cancer in the tenth house. Examinations are mainly of the ninth house, but I have been convinced by experience that the fifth house is important in any matter which involves some kind of competition. However, at the time I judged it as a ninth house question, so the main significators are the Moon (querent) and Venus, ruler of the ninth house. I also considered Mars because he was in the ninth house and close to the cusp.

The Moon applies well to both Mars and Venus, but before perfecting her aspect with these two she first has to deal with a sextile aspect with Saturn. Since the aspect was a sextile and not a square, conjunction or opposition, I thought that it would not interfere with the perfection of the sextile between the main significators — Moon and Venus. I therefore judged that the querent would pass his examinations and go to university. Some of my friends disagreed, arguing that it would not be as straightforward as that. Obviously I had taken a risk by giving a judgement with Saturn conjunct the Ascendant, but I argued for the power of the main significators, the Moon and Venus both dignified by sign.

In the event, the querent was obliged to resit one paper, and although he was not actually denied a place at a university, he decided to play safe and accept a place at a local polytechnic.

So I was nearly right but not quite. The effect of Saturn here was to reduce the degree of success promised elsewhere in the chart. He did pass his examinations with difficulty, and although he gained a place at an institution of higher learning, it could hardly be called a university. The querent seems to have settled for the minimum his father would put up with.

After he had been at college for two years pursuing an HND in business studies, he again asked a question, shown in Figure 46: Will I pass my examinations?

As will be seen, he's done it to me again. Strictly speaking the

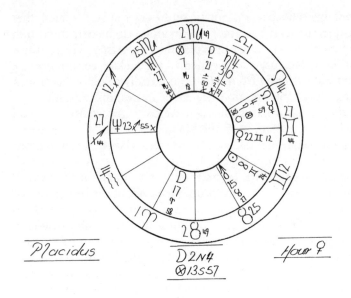

Figure 46.
Will I pass my examinations?
29 May 1981 9PM35 GMT 51N46 0W28

chart is not radical because more than 27 degrees rise at the Ascendant. It is too late to say. However, it so happens that I can find an excuse for judging this chart: the nativity of the querent is powerfully related to the horary, the natal Venus; Saturn and Moon all fall within a degree of the horary Ascendant. When this kind of contact occurs between a nativity and horary I usually judge the chart, and I did so in this case.

The querent admitted that he had done very little work in preparation for his examinations, but he had a good term work record and hoped that he had absorbed enough knowledge to carry him through — an attitude not unknown among Sagittarians.

Our first task is to sort out the significators. The querent is shown by Jupiter, and the examinations by Venus, lady of the ninth house. The Moon is co-ruler of the querent, and Saturn and Pluto must be considered because they occupy the ninth house.

Having appointed the significators we must now see if any relationship exists between them. Venus and Jupiter are not in aspect;

they have enjoyed a sextile relationship but that aspect has long passed. We must therefore focus our attention upon the Moon and Venus, and you will see that they apply by sextile aspect. That is a good sign, but the Moon must make an opposition with Pluto before completing her sextile with Venus. So it is not straightforward. Success is promised by the Moon going to Venus, but Pluto represents a barrier which must be crossed before the matter can be brought to a happy conclusion. We must attempt to discover what the nature of the interference symbolized by Pluto might be.

In horary astrology I do not find the outer planets consistent or easy to explain. However, I have two possibilities in mind: Pluto could represent some peculiar condition or circumstance which delays the final result, such as industrial action on the part of the examiners, the loss of papers, etc., or it could symbolize a person in authority who attempts to frustrate the success of the querent. I tended to favour the latter explanation, and when I put this possibility to the querent he immediately identified a tutor who had told him that if his work became the subject of a vote as to whether he would be awarded his diploma or not, he would vote against. Apparently these two had often clashed and they detested each other.

We must now ask ourselves whether the influence of this person is powerful enough to deny the querent his success. Pluto is retrograde and in a cadent house. He is disposed of by Venus, lady of the quesited, and she is coming angular. So my judgement is that although he might attempt to frustrate he does not succeed.

Let's take a closer look at Jupiter, ruler of the querent. He is just approaching the cusp of the ninth house and will shortly cross over it and make a conjunction with Saturn. Jupiter has only lately moved from retrograde motion to direct. This is to the advantage of the querent, and before the results are known Saturn will also move direct. Does this conjunction augur well or ill for the querent? Saturn is exalted in Libra and Jupiter is strong in his own ninth house. Bearing in mind that Saturn is the ruler of Capricorn, the natural tenth sign, I would say that this conjunction nicely symbolizes the querent gaining his qualification, for qualifications are a tenth house matter.

The End of the Matter for the querent is shown by the fourth house. Venus is lady of the fourth, and she is strong because she is angular. I like the position of Fortuna at the Midheaven, which often indicates success. Now a further complication may be seen by Venus closely applying to an opposition of Neptune, but in my experience Neptune more often than not causes worry on the part of the querent, and in this case I am inclined to think that it repeats the indication given by Moon opposition Pluto.

On balance my judgement was that the querent would pass his examinations by the skin of his teeth. He did get his qualification.

Figure 47: Will I get my degree?
A middle-aged lady had begun studying for an arts degree with the Open University and asked if she would eventually get her degree.

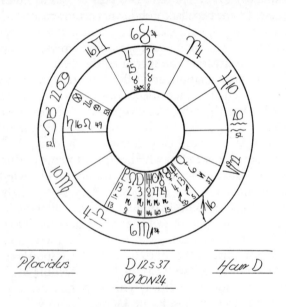

Figure 47.
Will I get my degree?
19 November 1976 10PM23 GMT 51N46 0W28

Once again we have the interesting situation of Saturn close to the Ascendant, a condition which is said to damage the question. In this case, however, he is not ill-conditioned and he is in the sign of his detriment, which reduces his power.

The significator of the querent is the Sun, and the significator of the quesited is Mars, ruler of the ninth. The Sun applies closely to a conjunction of Mars in the fourth house, so both planets are angular and Mars is also strong in Scorpio. This applying conjunction is a promise of perfection, but Mars changes sign before the actual conjunction can be made, so strictly this perfection is denied by refranation.

Another approach, however, is to consider the main reason why the lady wishes to obtain a degree, she does not want it to improve her employment prospects; her chief reason is status. Status is a tenth house matter, and the lady of the tenth is Venus. The Moon, co-ruler of the querent, applies immediately to a sextile of Venus in the sign of Capricorn (the tenth sign), in the fifth (competitive) house. This contact promises success.

There is a controversial reception between fourth house Mars and tenth house Jupiter (universal co-significator of the quesited), for Mars can go to the tenth house of his exaltation, and Jupiter can move to fourth house of his exaltation. This reception assists, and I took it to tip the balance in favour of the querent. So, notwithstanding Saturn at the Ascendant, I judged she would get her degree.

The querent stuck to her studies, producing consistently good results. Finally, in the autumn of 1981, she obtained her degree. She is now continuing her studies with the object of getting a higher degree.

14.
CAREER AND STATUS

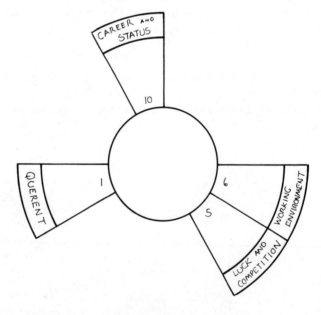

Universal co-significator of career and status: ⊙ ♄
Significator of the public: ☽
Natural sign of career and status: ♑

Figure 48.   Career and Status

An infinite variety of questions fall under this general heading. There are questions about career, about the possibility of getting a certain job, and also about critical situations that arise at one's place of employment. People ask about the viability of various business propositions, or the wisdom of following a certain course of action. Then there are queries related to status, such as achieving some kind of coveted position or office, or about being elected to a council, etc.

Obviously the tenth house is of great importance when judging such questions, as is the sign of Capricorn. The sixth house can have much to say about actual conditions at one's place of work, and the fifth house is worthy of serious consideration, particularly with questions that have to do with election to public office. Saturn, as natural ruler of tenth house matters should always be taken into account, but for all questions connected with elections the Moon is extremely potent, because she symbolizes the general public or electorate.

Figure 49: Will I get the job?
First of all let me show you a very straightforward chart. It is not one of my questions, but the first horary question of a young lady student of astrology, Lynn Choudry of Ilford, to whom I am grateful for permission to use it here.

The ruler of the querent is the Moon because Cancer rises; the ruler of the quesited is Jupiter, because Pisces is upon the cusp of the tenth house. So we have the Moon for Lynn and Jupiter for the job.

In this case we have a perfect example of perfection. The Moon applies by trine to Jupiter. She applies immediately; there is no impedition; there is nothing to stop the two primary significators coming together in harmonious aspect. So there is nothing to prevent the querent getting the job, and get the job she did. You will be interested to know that the job was in a hospital, most appropriate with the sign of hospitals (Pisces) upon the Midheaven.

This is a lovely example of a simple, straightforward horary chart. There is only one answer: 'Yes, you will get the job.' It is a strange fact that genuine students of astrology seem to attract charts that coincide with the level of their understanding of the art. It is not unusual for a first horary question to be simple and free from complication.

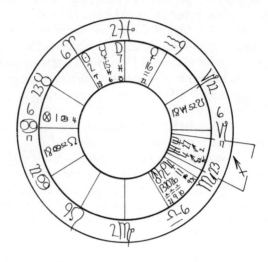

Figure 49. Will I get the job? 23 March 1982 No time recorded
E. London

Figure 50: Will I get the job?
In this case a mature lady made an application to become a prison
officer. The primary significators are the Sun for the querent and
Venus for the quesited.

The Sun and Venus are in no aspect with each other, but if we
move to the Moon as co-significator of the querent, we can see that
she will eventually make a sextile aspect with Venus. However, before
she can perfect that aspect, she must go through a square of Mercury,
the Sun and Neptune. Three bodies impedite the Moon, so it is
doubtful whether the matter can be successfully resolved. The Moon
might be able to surmount Mercury, and perhaps even Neptune,
but not the square with the Sun, for neither Sun nor Moon have
dignity; nor are they angular or in mutual reception. Another
consideration is that the Moon is within a degree of the fixed star
Fomalhaut, which generously confers 'malevolence of sublime
scope'.

The End of the Matter is ruled by Mars. He is powerful in the
fourth house, and although the Moon can make a trine aspect with

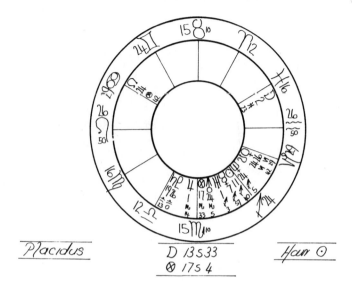

Placidus D 13s33 Hour ☉
⊗ 17s 4

Figure 50. Will I get the job? 3 December 1981 10PM00 GMT E. London

him, she is again impedited by the preceding square with the Sun.
I had to give an answer Yea or Nay, and I said Nay. The querent
did not get the job.

Figure 51: Will I have a musical career?
A young man involved with a small pop group in his spare time
but with a dream of becoming successful and professional, asked
the above question.

It is interesting to find Neptune, which is often associated with
music, at the Midheaven, but he is squared by the Sun, Fortuna
and the Nodes. Nonetheless Neptune nicely describes the dream.
The primary significators are Saturn for the querent and Mars for
the quesited, and they are not in aspect. The Moon is effectively
Void of Course, so nothing is likely to come of the matter. If any
doubt remains, Serpentis is at the Midheaven. Nothing prospers
under the ray of this evil degree, so the answer to the question is
a firm No.

The young man has now embarked on a permanent career in a
more secure area.

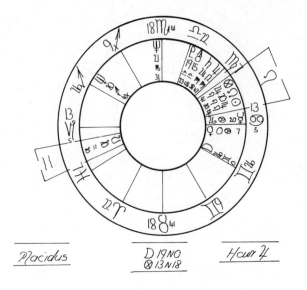

Placidus   D 19 NO   Hour 4
                    ⊗ 13 N 18

Figure 51. Will I have a musical career? 6 August 1980 6PM5 GMT
                         51N46 0W28

Figure 52: Whether to accept the proposition?
Two lady friends had a mutual interest in catering. One of them
learned that a catering concession in a local museum had become
vacant. She wanted to know if the querent would combine with
her in submitting a tender for the concession. The querent then
posed the above question.

The horary chart repeats the querent's natal angles; she is shown
by the Sun. In this case I would give the quesited to the fifth house,
for it is essentially a speculative venture. The fifth house is strongly
tenanted, but its primary significator is Mars. The lady who put the
proposition is a friend of the querent and a friend is normally shown
by the eleventh house, but in this case we are really concerned with
a *partnership,* so it is a seventh house matter. The significator of
the querent's friend is therefore Saturn.

The Sun in the seventh separates from the fifth house Jupiter-
Uranus conjunction, and applies widely to a good aspect of Fortuna,
but does little else. The Moon, co-ruler of the querent, does apply
widely to a trine of Mars, ruler of the quesited, but she cannot meet

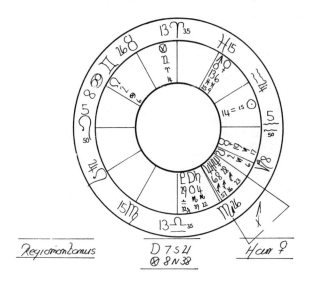

Figure 52. Whether to accept the proposition? 3 February 1983 3PM49
GMT 51N46 0W28

him without first passing through a conjunction with Saturn, and
even then as she trines Mars she immediately goes on to square the
Sun. Although Saturn is the significator of the friend, or perhaps
more properly of the proposed partnership, I did read him as
obstructive, and I did not like the fact that the Moon was besieged
between two malefics.

The querent would have had to give up a lucrative job in order
to take up this proposition. I did not think she would do so, since
both Sun and Moon are in fixed signs, and whatever else Saturn
represents here, he also testifies to extreme caution on the part of
the querent. I decided Saturn and the besiegement would prevent
the querent pursuing the matter. She carefully weighed the financial
implications and set her conclusions against the benefits of her present
job. In the end she decided to refuse the proposition.

Figure 53: Will I get the job?
I include this example because the chart is interesting for the degree
of its maleficity; it is a horrible chart.

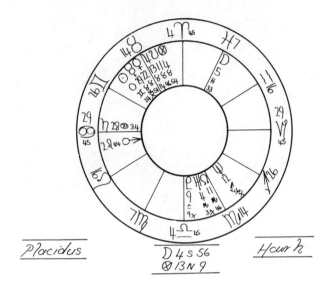

Placidus   D 4 S 56   Hour ♄
                  ⊗ 13 N 9

Figure 53.   Will I get the job? 21 May 1976 8AM21 GMT 51N33 0W6

I was considering answering an advertisement for an administrative post at an airport. I was qualified for the job and optimistic about securing it, then I drew the horary. Despite its adverse message I decided to go through with the matter, and I was granted an interview.

I arrived at the airport in plenty of time for my appointment but was kept waiting. When called in for interview I was accused of being late. The interviewing board consisted of about ten people. It was chaired by a pompous elderly man (he had the air of a local politician), and he was most aggressive. I was given no opportunity to express myself and the whole procedure was more in the nature of a dismissal rather than an interview. It seemed to me that the matter was already 'cut and dried' and that the interview was part of the procedure of 'going through the motions' on the part of the Airport Authority. Needless to say I did not get the job.

With Saturn on the Ascendant a horary question is damaged. Thirty degrees of Cancer rise; thus the matter is too late to judge. Upon these considerations alone the answer is No. However, the

Moon is my significator and she is not at all badly aspected, applying well to Jupiter, Venus and Mercury — and even to the rising Saturn. But these are hollow promises and avail nothing against the vandalism of Saturn's hammer.

Mercury is retrograde, a condition that warns the astrologer that: (a) he is not in possession of all the relevant information; or (b) he will change his mind about the matter enquired about. In this case (a) is appropriate, and combined with the effect of the late rising degree, my suspicion that the matter had already been decided is confirmed. Mercury is also conjunct the degree of the malefic fixed star Alcyone (the Weeping Sisters), always a bad indication.

The Moon and Jupiter are in mutual reception. It is interesting that a former superior of mine, at that time someone with influence in the industry, tried to assist me in this matter. Jupiter is conjunct the eleventh house (friends), but also close to the South Node. It is possible that his attempts to assist proved counter-productive.

Finally, Mercury and the Sun are within orbs of conjunction, although the aspect is disassociate so that it is not a true combustion, Mercury is still Under Sunbeams, a weakening condition which may well have been responsible for my inability to express myself at the interview.

I asked the question 'Will I get the job?' The chart replied 'No.' The question is irrelevant (Saturn rising) because the matter has already been decided (late degree rising), and you are not in possession of all the facts (Mercury retrograde).

Figure 54: The interview
Useful information can often be found in charts drawn for the time of interview. Such charts should be treated broadly, but not strictly, in a horary way. An interview chart is not a question; it is a *significant moment,* and its potential may be explored. We do not give great importance to the degree rising; whether it is early or late seems to make little difference. The Ascendant represents the interviewee and the Descendant the interviewer. One of the best indications is when the significator of the interviewee and the significator of the interviewer are in good aspect. This shows that they will agree and feel at harmony with one another. The applying aspects of the Moon are important for they show how the matter will develop. The astrologer should weigh the various indications and make a

judgement or give advice based upon his knowledge and experience. It should be remembered that interview charts are helpful, but overriding importance should be given to the horary.

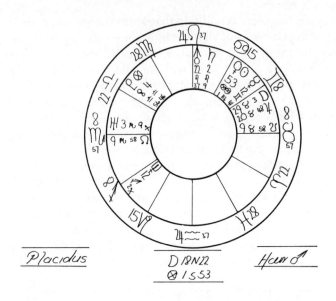

Figure 54. The interview 24 June 1976 3PM45 GMT 53N30 2W15

The chart shows Mars for the interviewee and Venus for the interviewer. They are not in aspect; there is no meaningful relationship between them. The Moon is Void of Course, which is not an indication of success, and she also occupies the degree of the evil fixed star Alcyone. There is little here to give encouragement.

Figure 55: Will Peter lose his job?
A large company for which I was working bought a number of shops from a small company, and with the shops came Peter. Peter was a man in his mid-fifties, slightly disabled following a motor accident some years before. He was a good-natured man with a great deal of energy. Part of the deal was that the large company undertook to give Peter a job within their organization. He was put to work assisting me. At first I was apprehensive, but I very quickly grew to like the man and we worked very well together. Several months

passed and I was shocked to learn that the company was thinking of getting rid of Peter. Their excuse was that his disability made it impossible for him to do his job, which was absolute nonsense, but actually (I found out later) they were afraid of compensation claims if his disability became worse. Peter was worried about the situation, and I was angry. The question occurred to me, 'Will Peter lose his job?'

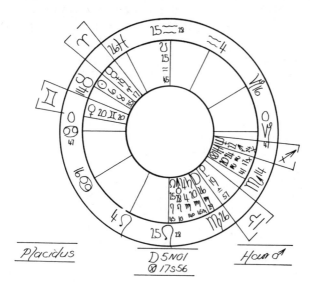

Figure 55. Will Peter lose his job? 26 April 1980 7AM35 GMT
51N46 0W28

The first degree of Cancer rises; the chart is premature; it is too early to say. The Moon is Void of Course: nothing will come of the matter.

Now it was I who asked the question, Peter was a colleague and we were friendly; thus he must be shown by the eleventh house. Peter's significator is Jupiter; the significator of his job is Saturn. They are both in the sixth house, but they are 16 degrees from a conjunction. That conjunction did not perfect until a long time afterwards and even then it occurred in the following sign of Libra. The Sun (ruler of the sixth), separates from a trine of Jupiter. Apart from that, Jupiter is on his own. Peter is alone and friendless, I thought, trapped in the sixth house, a prisoner of his health condition. A dilemma arose in the judgement of this chart. It is premature and the Moon is Void of Course. If I give priority to a Void of Course Moon, the answer is, 'Nothing will come of it,' and the implication of such an answer is that Peter will not lose his job. But if I give priority to the rising degree, I must judge: 'It is too early to say.' In fact I reasoned that if a question is premature, it is not possible to say that nothing will come of it. I decided to await developments.

The following month the matter came to prominence again, because it became certain that the company had decided to get rid of Peter. I was furious, and thought that if he took advice he might well have a case against the company. I promised that I would give evidence to any tribunal that he was more than capable of doing his job, and I also let my superior know I would do so. In the midst of my indignation I posed the question: 'If he fights, will he win?'

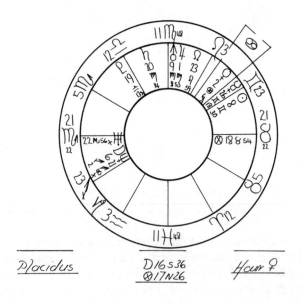

Figure 56. If he fights will he win? 29 May 1980 6PM25 GMT 51N46 0W28

Look at the chart. My significator is Mars; there I am, flashing my sword at the company at the Midheaven full of Virgoan righteous indignation, and directly invoking the magic of astrology (Uranus) at the Ascendant. With the Moon in Sagittarius square Mars and opposing the Sun, I was definitely 'jumping out of my pram'.

I calmed down enough to note that this was a radical chart. Peter must again be shown by the eleventh house. Imagine that the eleventh cusp rises, and we may better see Peter's position. There he is, Venus in Cancer, intercepted in the tenth house and retrograde. He didn't look very aggressive to me. The Moon in Sagittarius going at once to an opposition of the Sun did not look very promising; nor did I like the Moon's following square aspect with Mars in Virgo. The company (as far as Peter is concerned) is ruled by the eighth house of the chart. Mercury is their significator, strong in Gemini and close to the cusp of Peter's tenth. So Peter looked weak and the company strong. Peter did not seem to be able to win, but he didn't look willing to fight either. When I spoke to him about it, it became apparent that he was not going to make an issue of the matter, so I subsided and accepted the inevitable.

Yet, consider Venus again. She is in Cancer — a mute, devious and secretive sign. Cancers are not known for meeting problems head-on. They prefer a sideways approach, and Cancers are certainly not going to tell anyone else their business. And if there was any reason to think that this Cancer was different, the interception and retrogradation dispel all doubt. This Venus equals secrecy cubed.

Now see what she is up to: she is retrograding quietly back to a sextile with Jupiter. It seems that Peter, faced with the situation, played his own canny game. He agreed with the company that he probably could not do his job properly because of his disability, and he received a generous severance payment. He then went back to work for the company who had sold him in the first place. So the matter ended quite well for him — Venus (Peter) sextile Jupiter (lord of the End of the Matter). Not for the first time in my life I 'got out of my pram' for nothing. This case also shows the stupidity of sticking one's astrological nose into other people's affairs without being asked to do so — but it is most interesting astrology.

Election to Public Office
My wife embraces local politics with a similar passion to that which

I give to astrology. Politicians, local and national, are a peculiar breed, for the most part obsessed with the desire to hold on to their office at all costs. I have not noticed much sympathy for astrology amongst them, but now and again (usually around election times), some of them become so possessed with the fear of rejection that I get accosted in the favourite corner of my local pub and asked an astrological question. Sometimes they even buy me a drink. Thus I probably have more than my fair share of questions related to elections, etc.

Figure 57: Will I retain the chairmanship?

Local politicians, by virtue of their office, are often seconded to serve on a variety of other local bodies which spend public money. Chief in importance among these are the governing boards of schools. The querent, a local councillor, had been Chairman of the Board of Governors of a local school for a number of years. She enjoyed the position and had a good relationship with the staff. Due to certain changes on the Board, which changed the political complexion slightly, she was afraid that a coup would be organized against her in order to deprive her of the chairmanship.

The querent is shown by Mars, very powerful at the Ascendant and looking remarkably like he is prepared to do bloody battle. Although Mercury is nominally lord of the tenth house (this is a status matter), I was impressed by Jupiter at the Midheaven and I saw him as symbolizing the chairmanship. Mars and Jupiter are in very close applying sextile, and it looked to me as if the querent would be very difficult to dislodge. If we take Mercury as lord of the tenth and the Moon as co-ruler of the querent, then we also have them applying by sextile without interruption, another indication that the querent will retain the chairmanship.

The querent's opponent must be shown by the seventh house. Venus, lady of the seventh, is cadent and weak in Virgo; she applies to nothing and can be no danger to the querent. Furthermore the cusp of the seventh is upon the malefic fixed star degree Caput Algol, which is not good for the opponent.

The querent did retain the chairmanship; her opponent did not turn up at the Annual General Meeting of the Governing Board. I must say that I have always found, when Mars is at the Ascendant and not badly aspected, it is a powerful argument that the querent will win any contest.

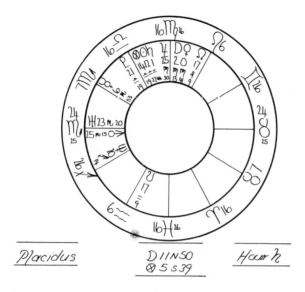

Figure 57. Will I retain the chairmanship? 5 October 1980 10AM15 GMT
51N46 0W28

Figure 58: Will I be elected?

This question came from a young man who had not been elected before, having tried on a number of occasions without success.

His significator is Mars. As I have explained, elections involve both the tenth house (status) and the fifth house (competitions), and this chart confirms this by putting the Sun (ruler of the tenth) in the fifth. The ruler of the querent is weak in Taurus and cadent, and he also opposes Saturn which is too close to the Ascendant for comfort. On the other hand, the Moon (co-ruler of the querent), applies immediately to the Sun in the fifth house and is in no way impeded.

As we have seen elsewhere, when Saturn is close to the Ascendant he can have the effect of diminishing the degree of success if success is shown in the chart. In this case there are 9 degrees between Saturn and the Ascendant. He is not close enough to destroy or damage the question, but he might diminish the degree of success. However, I have always held that a good applying aspect between the Lights is a very powerful indication of success. So I told the querent that

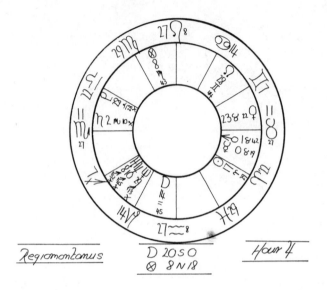

Figure 58. Will I be elected? 7 April 1983 8PM57 GMT 51N46 0W28

he would be elected, but that his majority would probably be less than he anticipated. He was elected with a respectable majority, but it was less than he had calculated.

It is worth reflecting that if I had entered the pub in which this question was asked half an hour earlier, Saturn would have been retrograde upon the Ascendant and I would have had to judge that he would not be elected.

Figure 59: Will I be elected?
Political parties usually put up candidates for seats (local or national) when they know they have no chance of winning. They do it to 'show the flag'. The querent in this case had agreed to stand for a council seat which was normally safe for the opposition. She began to campaign, and as she got into the fight she became optimistic. This is not unusual; nobody can really fight well unless they believe they're going to win, and when touched by the fever of battle they do believe that they will win, no matter how hopeless it may seem to a detached observer.

The significator of the querent is the Sun, and the Sun in Aries

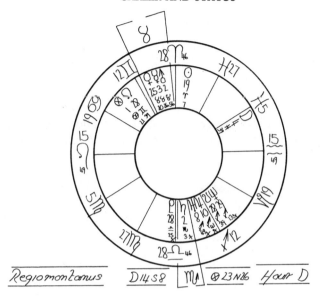

Figure 59. Will I be elected? 9 April 1983 0PM40 GMT 51N46 0W28

in this chart well describes the positive and aggressive manner in which she approached the campaign. Again we must take note of the tenth and fifth houses when considering the quesited. Mars rules the tenth and he is in the tenth, but he is weak by sign and in no aspect to the Sun. Jupiter rules the fifth; he is strong by sign and close to the fifth cusp, but the Sun separates from a good aspect of Jupiter.

Since there is no aspect between the primary significators, let's turn to the Moon as co-ruler of the querent. She is just separating from a sextile of Mars and applying to a square of Jupiter, so there are no good applying aspects between the significators, no matter how they are viewed.

If we look to the fourth house to see how the matter will end, we find Saturn close to the cusp, which is not encouraging, and although Venus (ruler of the fourth) is dignified by sign and elevated, she does occupy the degrees of the malefic fixed star, Caput Algol. My judgement was that the querent would not be elected, but I did not tell the querent in this case. She was so caught up in her campaign I had no wish to dishearten her. The ruler of the seventh is retrograde, another example of the artist not actually delivering judgement when his significator is retrograde.

The result was very interesting: the querent failed to secure election by a margin of less than ten votes after three recounts.

Figure 60: Will he be elected?
At the 1983 General Election I was particularly interested in the likely result for a highly marginal seat. The candidate in whom I was interested did not ask me a question as I hoped he would, so I asked the question myself — 'Will he be elected?'

Since I am asking a question about the affairs of another with whom I have no particular relationship, he will be shown by the seventh house. His opponent in the election must be shown by the seventh from the seventh, which is the first house of the chart. The electorate as always, is signified by the Moon. This was in fact a three-cornered fight, but when I asked the question, I had in my mind only two people: the person I was talking about — the Conservative candidate — and his Socialist opponent. The Social Democratic Party also had a candidate but I did not think about him at the time.

The Conservative is signified by Mercury, and the Socialist by Jupiter. Both are retrograde, but Jupiter is strong by sign. The fifth house of the Conservative (the eleventh of the chart) is ruled by Mars, and the fifth house of his opponent by Venus. Now this is not an easy chart; there are conflicting testimonies. But in the end two factors led me to judge that the Conservative would win. As I have said, the Moon represents the electorate, so in questions of this kind her influence is crucial. Whatever the Moon is going to do in the chart must symbolize what the voters are going to do. In this chart she immediately makes a square with Mars and then goes on to square Jupiter and his companion Uranus. There is a suggestion here that the voters will reject the opposition, but what sealed my judgement was the reception between the Moon and Mercury (significator of the man I asked about). The electorate and the Conservative are in good relationship with each other because of the reception. I therefore judged that the Conservative would win because his opponent would lose.

In the event, the Socialist and SDP voters split the overall opposition vote and allowed the Conservative to win with a

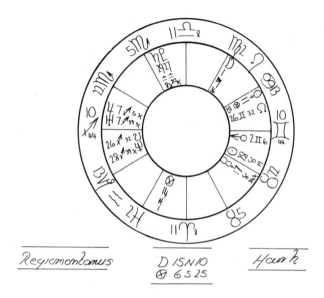

Figure 60.   Will he be elected? 19 May 1983 8PM55 GMT 51N46 0W28

comfortable majority. Once again we have the ruler of the seventh
retrograde. I did not give my judgement to the Conservative
candidate — he wasn't interested in my judgements.

Now it is very interesting that the Moon applies to a square of
Jupiter and then Uranus close to the first cusp. At the time of the
question I did not seriously consider the SDP candidate, but the
Socialist was a well-known left-winger from the GLC, and he would
be well described by Uranus. If we take Jupiter and Uranus as
symbolizing the SDP candidate and the Socialist respectively, then
the Moon rejects (square) first Jupiter and then Uranus, and Jupiter
is strong by sign. The voters in fact placed the SDP candidate second
in the poll and the Socialist a poor third.

15.
LOSS AND THEFT

I think that questions concerning loss and theft present the astrologer with the greatest challenge of all. There are many rules laid down by the old astrologers for the judgement of such questions. I shall attempt to cover these rules here, but as I have repeatedly tried to demonstrate, such rules should be taken for guidance rather than as articles of faith.

Lost or Stolen
If something is lost and one is not sure whether it has been stolen, it is sensible to see what the chart has to say on the subject. The querent is obviously shown by the Ascendant; generally the lost property is shown by the second house; and a thief is shown by the seventh house. Lost property may also be shown by the Moon, the dispositor of the Moon, and the fourth house ruler or a planet in the fourth is also important when attempting to find something lost in the home.

When you are unsure of whether a thing has been stolen or not, the main consideration is whether the significator of the thief is afflicting the querent or the property of the querent. A thief's significator is usually the ruler of the seventh, but it can also be a *peregrine planet in an angle*, or a planet in the seventh. So, if the significator of the thief is in the first house, or in bad aspect to, or disposing of the Moon, it is an indication that the goods have been stolen. If the significator of the querent's property is in the seventh, or if the lord of the seventh or a malefic planet afflicts any of the significators of the property, it is an argument of theft.

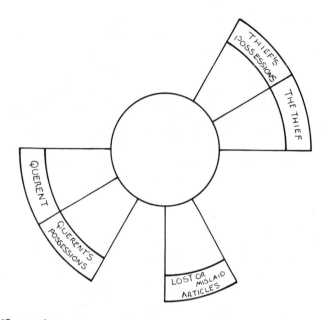

Significator of things lost or stolen: ☽
Significator of a thief: 7th Ruler/Peregrine Planet

Figure 61.   Loss and Theft.

Recovery

To discover whether something lost will be found, consider the following. The Moon applying to the lord of the Ascendant; the Moon applying to her dispositor; the Moon in the Ascendant and applying to the lord of the twelfth; the Moon in the Ascendant or the second house. When the Moon's dispositor is in the third, or in sextile aspect with the Ascendant, there is hope of finding the lost article; if the Moon's dispositor separates from the lord of the sixth, eighth or twelfth, and applies to the second cusp or the Moon, there is also hope of finding the thing; if the Moon is well aspected by Jupiter or Venus, the lost thing has probably been found by someone of good character who would like to restore it, and if the Moon or one of the benefics aspect the Ascendant, it will be restored.

Tradition states that if none of these conditions are present the lost article will not be recovered.

To determine whether something stolen will be recovered, see whether the querent looks fortunate in the chart, if he and his property show signs of coming together, or if benefics or the Sun or Moon are in fortunate relationship with the significators of his property, and judge accordingly. It should be said that if the second house or its ruler are afflicted, if the lord of the seventh is in the eighth, if malefics are in the Ascendant, or if the Sun and the Moon are below the horizon, then it argues that the stolen goods will not be recovered. When attempting to find *when* something may be found or recovered, see how many degrees separate the querent from the significator of his property and judge according to the Generally Accepted Measure of Time.

If the Thief will be Apprendended
Consider his significator. The more afflicted it is, the more unfortunate the aspects he will encounter, the more likely he is to be taken. The more fortunate it is, the more fortunate the aspects he will encounter, the more likely he is to get away with it.

Relationship of the Thief to the Querent
Consider the house occupied by the significator of the thief and judge accordingly. For example, if it is in the fifth, the thief might be a child of the querent; in the sixth, a servant; in the seventh, a spouse, etc.

Where to Look for Lost Property
The various combinations are numerous. The astrologer really has to consider his options, take into account the individual circumstances of the question, and apply his common sense to the chart. If you know a thing is lost within a room, there is no point in looking for it in the rest of the house; if it is lost within the house, there is no point in looking for it in the garden. For the direction in which something may lie, be guided by the directions by sign given in Chapter 9 — Figure 19.

The traditional way of judging general location is to see if the significator of the querent and the significator of the thing lost are in the same quarter of the chart, or if the Moon and the significator of the querent are in the same quarter. If they are, and not more than 30 degrees apart, the thing is in the home of the owner, or very close to it; between 30 degrees and 70 degrees, it is the town where the owner lives; but if they are not in the same quarter, the lost thing is far away.

For things lost within a house one may also see if the ruler of the second is in an angle, and some idea of where it is may be taken from the angle occupied. In the first house, it is in the room most frequently used by the querent, or somewhere in which he keeps his personal possessions; in the fourth house, it is in the middle of the building, or in its oldest part, or in a room which elderly people most frequent; in the seventh house, it is in the room where the querent's spouse spends most time; in the tenth house, it is in the most public room of the house — the lounge, dining-room or living-room.

To discover the kind of place where a lost article may be found, consider the significators: the lord of the Ascendant, the lord of the second, the Moon and Fortuna. See the quality of the sign in which most of them are placed. If Air signs predominate, the lost thing is hidden high up in the house or room. If Water signs predominate, it is near water, maybe in a bathroom, kitchen or wash-house. If most of the significators are in Fire signs, then it is near heat or fire, or near the walls of the house or room. With Earth signs prevalent, it is on or near the floor.

If the property is outside of the house, Air signs suggest it is in the garden, orchard or field, above ground level or upon the highest part of the ground. Fire signs suggest it is near the walls of the house. Water signs suggest it is near water. Earth signs suggest it is near a bridge of the entrance to the property upon which the house stands.

If the significators are just changing sign, the suggestion is that the lost thing is behind something, between two rooms or near the entrance to a room. It will be higher or lower in the place according to the nature of the sign: Air — high up; Earth — low down; and Fire — midway.

When looking further afield than the confines of the home for something that is lost, consider the Moon; if she is in a human sign it is where men frequent; if in a bestial sign it is where beasts frequent. If the Moon is in a Fire sign, it is near fire, or where fire has been, or upon hills or high ground. If she is in a Water sign, it is near water. Cancer denotes pure or running water; Scorpio dirty or polluted water; and Pisces stagnant water or some other liquid. If she is in an Air sign, it is on open ground or near windows or garrets. If in an Earth sign, she denotes earthy places, mud and clay. If the Moon, or her dispositor are in cardinal signs, it indicates newly built areas, or hills and dales. In a fixed sign, plain and level ground. In a common sign, near water, or on low wet ground. The cardinal signs also denote high places, roofs, ceilings, etc.; the fixed signs denote upon the ground, under the earth, near walls, etc.; the common signs denote ditches, pits, and market places; but Water signs also indicate cellars and the foundations of buildings.

William Lilly devised what he considered to be a most effective formula for finding lost articles within a house: Take the sign Ascending, the sign of the lord of the Ascendant, the sign on the fourth cusp, the sign of the Moon, the sign on the second cusp, the sign of the ruler of the second, the sign of Fortuna, and the sign of the ruler of Fortuna. Consider the sign most prevalent amongst these and what direction that sign suggests (Chapter 9 — Figure 19).

Having found the appropriate quarter of heaven, the predominant element shows the kind of place in the house where the lost thing is most likely to be found: Air signs — above ground; Fire signs — near a wall or partition; Earth signs — on the floor; Water signs — near water or in a moist place.

Figure 62: Where are my rings?
This example and the one following come from Carole Barnes of Ilford, who posed the questions, drew the charts and made a judgement. I am most grateful for her permission to use them.

The querent and her second house are ruled by the Sun. If we give the Moon to the querent and the Sun to the rings, we can see that the Moon is angular and applying at once to the Sun in the fifth house. The rings will be found because the querent and her rings are coming together. The fifth house is particularly important, not only because the significator of the rings occupies it, but also because the ruler of the fifth — Mars — is conjunct the Ascendant. If we use our common sense and ask what part of a house is signified by the fifth house, we must surely say: the bedroom.

The rings were found five days after the question was asked, although they were lost sixteen days before the question. The querent

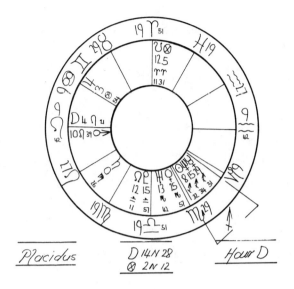

Figure 62.
Where are my rings?
30 November 1977 8PM35 GMT Ilford

found them while she was at a pottery class, in a box containing pottery materials. This box was kept in her bedroom, so at the time the question was asked they were actually in her bedroom. The fifth house also rules leisure activities (pottery classes).

Figure 63: Where is the envelope?
In this example Carole had lost an envelope containing some papers from the BBC. She is shown by the Moon. As we are considering a lost document, common sense would suggest that its significator should be shown by the ruler of the third or by Mercury, natural ruler of documents, rather than the ruler of the second house. The Sun in Taurus (ruler of the third) does not have the feel of documents about it, so one is left with Mercury, or possibly with Mars in the third house.

Mercury is in Aries applying to Pluto by opposition, Neptune by trine, Venus by sextile, and Mars by trine. After negotiating the opposition to Pluto, Mercury is entirely well-aspected. The Moon separates from a conjunction of Saturn, a sextile with Fortuna, and applies to a sextile with Uranus. She is in fact translating light between Fortuna and Uranus.

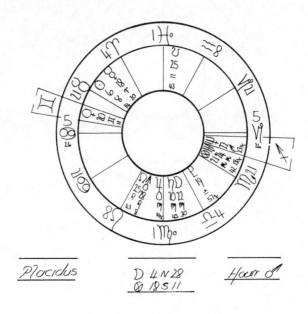

Placidus   ☽ 4 N 28   Hour ♂
            ☉ 18 S 11

Figure 63.
Where is the envelope?
26 April 1980 7AM54 GMT Ilford

Carole reasoned as follows: Aries = east; Fire signs suggest near a wall and at middle height. She thought the document was close to the east wall of the house, at mantlepiece level, near heat. She followed these directions in her lounge. She eventually found the document. It was on the east wall, in an astrology book, on a bookshelf at eye-level. But the most fascinating aspect of the find was that the astrology book was on a shelf just above a fish-tank with a pump and light, so the book was warm.

It is very nice to find Mercury applying to Neptune (fish) and to Mars (heat), and it is also interesting that the Moon translates light between Fortuna and Uranus in Scorpio (water pump?). Pluto seems to have been of little consequence in this matter.

Figure 64: Where is my opal ring?
I was at the Astrological Association's Conference at Warwick
University, where I had given a talk on horary astrology. I was
approached by a lady who asked if she might pose a horary question.
I said, 'Of course.' She asked: 'Where is my opal ring?' We duly
noted the time and she asked me to attempt a judgement. The ring,
a present from her husband, had been put away somewhere 'safe'
by him and had not been seen since.

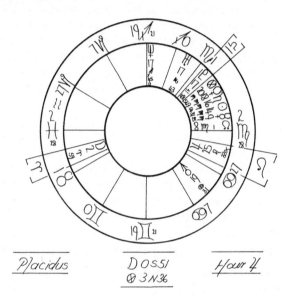

Figure 64.
Where is my opal ring?
7 September 1979 6PM15 GMT 52N23 1W34

The next day, Maggie Hyde, Gordon Watson, Jane Farrer and
myself got together to discuss the chart. Strictly speaking it was
invalid; less than 3 degrees rose, Mercury was combust, as was Venus
(natural ruler of jewellery), and Saturn was in the seventh house.
However, we were at an astrological conference and this chart was
a special challenge. It was also the lady's first horary question, so
we thought that the chart must be significant. We saw the early
rising degree as symbolizing the querent's lack of experience in horary

astrology, and the combust Mercury as her inability to judge the chart herself.

We pinpointed the ring as Mars in Cancer in the fifth house, it being an adornment rather than property (second house). This was an odd and crucial move. Why it was made is impossible to say; it just seemed appropriate at the time. The nature of the object and the property part of it seemed well covered by Venus being closely sextile Mars. Venus being combust in the seventh also appeared neatly to describe its lost condition and the husband's part in that loss. Now that I am older and wiser, I know that it is not invalid to see the lord of the sign of the Moon as a significator of a lost article.

We decided that the ring would be restored to the querent because Moon and Mars were in mutual reception, and also the Moon's final aspect was a trine with Jupiter (significator of the querent). We thought that the room where the ring would be found was likely to be a bedroom or similar (fifth house), and we thought that it would be near liquids (Cancer), probably toilet liquids, perfume perhaps, but because of the strong masculine element we finally settled on *male toiletries* (Gordon Watson liked 'Brut'). Later I gave the querent our judgement and at this point she told me that the ring had been missing for three years and promised to let me know if it turned up. I must confess I then wrote the matter off. No wonder, I said to myself, the chart was invalid. If they have been looking for it on and off for three years it is unlikely to turn up now!

Extract from the letter describing the finding of the ring
The ring had been found in a cupboard in her husband's dressing room.

'. . . Needless to say he'd sifted through all this lot several times since he mislaid the ring in 1975 but had found nothing. So today he's sifting through it again looking for some architect's plans and there sitting in an envelope was the ring as large as life. 'Where?' says I. 'Come and see' says he. 'Well' says I, 'It should be among masculine type toilet liquids, so what are all those bottles and jars and things?'

There was an empty miniature Cinzano bottle, a jar of hairdressing gel (not very masculine because it was a jar of jollop that I'd discarded and he's gathered up because he can't bear to throw anything away . . .).

But there was still another jar against which the envelope with the ring was wedged, and the label on it? 'Penis (Heat) Development Cream', made by the House of Pan. Now then, I'll bet you never thought of that interpretation for Mars in Cancer in the Fifth, did you!

So you were absolutely right in your judgement, all points being spot on except the time factor, which turned out to be sixty-three days instead of six or twenty-three' (which I had apparently suggested).

It is interesting to note that the ring was found when Venus made a conjunction with Neptune at the Midheaven of the horary chart.

In subsequent correspondence with the querent, she readily and generously agreed that I could include this fascinating case in my book, and I am most grateful for her kind permission.

Figure 65: Will I recover my wallet?

I was teaching astrology at evening classes in London. During the break I left my coat in the classroom, and later I discovered my wallet was missing. At first I wasn't really too sure whether I had lost it somehow, or whether it had been stolen. I soon became convinced that I had been the victim of a theft, and apparently such occurrences were not unusual at that particular school.

Venus, my significator, is upon the cusp of the seventh; I am therefore in the power of the thief or thieves. Mars, the ruler of my second house and therefore significator of my wallet, is also in the seventh, so it is in the hands of thieves. There would seem to have been three thieves — Venus, Mars and Mercury are all in the seventh, close together in Aries (children or young persons). They were probably all male, but perhaps two were male and one female.

One might say, since the significator of myself applies to the significator of my wallet by conjunction, that I would recover it, but the conjunction could not take place within the sign, so the promise of recovery is denied by refranation. There is only one good aspect to consider; the Moon applies to a sextile of Saturn (lord of the fourth), but she also goes on to oppose the Sun and conjunct Uranus in my second house upon the degree of the evil Serpentis. There is little sign of recovery, and I did not get it back. The thieves — Venus, Mars and Mercury — are all late in the sign; they apply to no bad aspects before moving into Taurus, so they were not caught.

Figure 66: Was it my son?

The querent had missed a number of items from her home, and she suspected that her son might have taken and sold them, so she asked the question.

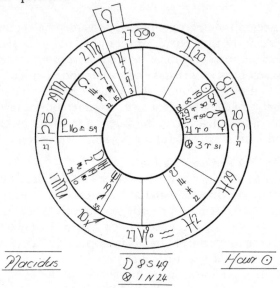

Maridus   𝄞 D 8s49   Hour ☉
                   ⊗ 1 N 24

Figure 65.
Will I recover my wallet?
10 May 1979 4PM45 GMT London

There are two powerful indications that her suspicions were justified. Firstly, Saturn — the significator of the thief is right upon the cusp of the fifth house (querent's children), and that seems clear enough. However, there is confirming evidence from the ruler of the fifth (Venus); she just separates from an aspect of Fortuna in the querent's second house.

The Moon (querent), applies well to Saturn, so she did not do anything about it, but the message of the chart seems clear.

Lost Animals

If a question is received about a lost pet or animal, the significators are: the ruler of the sixth for small animals and the ruler of the twelfth for large animals. The Moon should also be seen as a significator

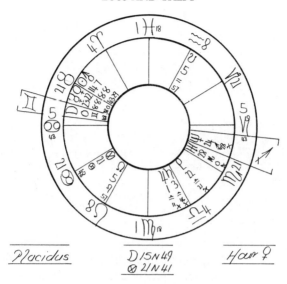

Figure 66.
Was it my son?
5 May 1981 7AM21 GMT London

of a missing animal. Isolate the appropriate significators and judge according to the foregoing rules for finding something that is lost.

To judge whether a lost animal is dead or not, follow these general rules. If the Moon applies to the ruler of the eighth house from the Moon, it is an indication that the animal is dead. If the dispositor of the Moon is likewise applying to the ruler of the eighth house from the Moon, it suggests the same. A further sign that the animal is dead is when the ruler of the eighth house of the chart has application from the Moon or her dispositor.

16.
SICKNESS AND DEATH

Times have changed somewhat since a sick doctor approached astrologer William Lilly to find out what was wrong with him. The modern astrologer may sometimes be asked a similar question: 'What is wrong with me?' But more often than not a querent will know the nature of his disease and he is more interested to know what will come of the matter; whether the illness is as serious as he has been led to believe; whether he will return to full health and when; if an operation is really necessary.

An astrologer should be very careful about trying to diagnose sickness. He should not attempt to act in a doctor's stead. You will know what parts of the body and what organs are traditionally ruled by the signs and houses, and it may well be possible for you to see a diagnosed ailment confirmed by the horary chart. You should certainly be able to judge whether a person is sick or not, whether the illness is serious or not, how long it is likely to last, and whether a full recovery may be expected. If a person is sick the chart must reflect it, for the body of the querent will be under attack. Those astrologers particularly interested in medical astrology should obtain a specialist book on the subject. I will not attempt to set out here the various astrological correlations with disease; such a project is worthy of a book to itself.

When one is asked about death one should proceed with great caution. There is a school of thought which holds that such questions should not be answered at all. You must decide upon each individual case you attract, whether you are competent to answer, and even if competent whether you *should* answer. Personally, I allow myself to be guided by the circumstances; I give judgement if I feel I must. No advice can be given on this matter; each astrologer must make his own decision.

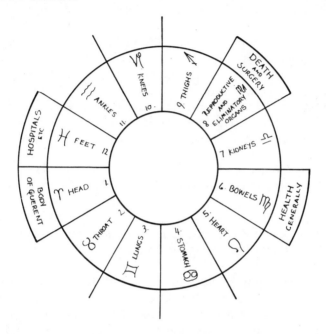

Figure 67. Sickness and Death

Sickness is primarily a sixth house and Virgo matter, but the Ascendant itself is important because it symbolizes the body. The twelfth house and Pisces must also be considered for they have dominion over hospitals, asylums, etc. The eighth house and Scorpio are mainly concerned with death, and the fourth house and Cancer can give indications about the end of life. Sometimes it may be necessary to consider all these areas in one question. If only for the purposes of testing their validity, it is as well to calculate the Part of Death and the Part of Sickness for all questions concerned with sickness and death.

The examples in this chapter attempt to move in stages from a condition of reasonable health to one of imminent death.

Figure 68: What will the chest X-ray reveal?
The querent had suffered from a worrying chest condition for some time; he just could not get rid of it. He was low, depressed and very worried. Finally the doctor decided that he should have a chest X-ray.

We want to know whether the querent is sick or not. It is interesting that the ruler of the querent, the Moon, is shown in the third house of enquiry just having moved into the sign of Virgo, signifying that the querent is enquiring about his health.

How do we discover whether the querent is sick or not? If a person is sick the chart must reflect it. It is the Ascendant that represents the body and the sixth house which has dominion over his state of health. These houses and / or their rulers may be expected to be under attack if the querent, or the person enquired about, is really sick.

A person is not sick if the Ascendant and the sixth house are unafflicted, or if the rulers of the first and sixth houses do not afflict each other, or are not themselves afflicted by Mars, Saturn or another malefic. Likewise if the Sun is in the sixth house, or the Moon is not afflicted in the eighth or twelfth houses. Similarly if the Moon is in good aspect with the ruler of the Ascendant; if Venus and Jupiter are in the first house or in good aspect with the cusps of the first or sixth.

These are traditional rules that are intended for guidance. In any question, the chart itself and what it says to the astrologer are of the greatest importance. A good general rule regarding sickness is: if there is no aspect between the ruler of the first and the ruler of the sixth, there is no sickness. Also, if the Moon is Void of Course, there is usually nothing to worry about.

In Figure 68, the Moon is ruler of the first and Jupiter is ruler of the sixth, and there is no aspect between them. Saturn is about to move out of the first house; Neptune is at the cusp of the sixth (which describes the worry of the querent); but Jupiter is applying to Neptune and the cusp of the sixth by trine. Venus is angular in the sign of health and in good aspect to the Ascendant, and the final aspect the Moon will make is a conjunction with that Venus. There is no sickness in this chart; the matter will end well — and so it did, the querent being told that there was nothing at all wrong with his chest.

Note the applying aspects of the Moon. She applies first by sextile to Mars in the twelfth house (the querent went to hospital); then by sextile to Uranus (the querent had an X-ray); then by sextile to the Sun in the fifth house (there was nothing wrong with the querent).

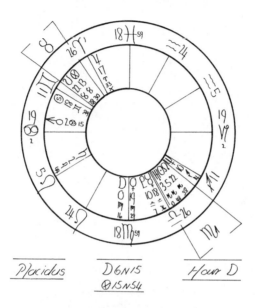

Figure 68. What will the chest X-ray reveal? 29 October 1975
8PM50 GMT 51N33 0W11

Here is another example of a good applying aspect between the Lights ending well for the querent. On her path to perfect a sextile with the Sun, the Moon encounters no difficult aspects with any other body. So the matter ended well, with the querent being told that his health was perfect (Moon conjunct Venus in Virgo).

The Part of Sickness is in Gemini in the twelfth house; the querent *thought* he had a *chest* problem.

Figure 69: *What ails my sister?*
The person who asked this question knows quite a bit about astrology. She was in the habit of telephoning her sister from time to time for a general chat. One day she rang and was answered by her brother-in-law, who said that his wife was ill and could not come to the phone. Indeed he was very worried about her because for the past week she

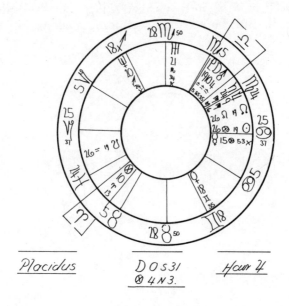

Placidus   D 0 S 31   Hour ♃
                  ⊗ 4 N 3.

Figure 69(a). What ails my sister? 18 July 1980 8PM0 GMT London

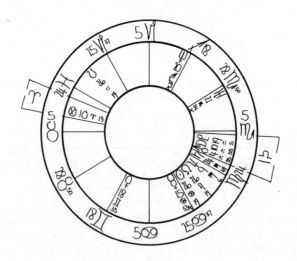

Figure 69(b). Chart turned to show 3rd cusp rising

had been sitting in a chair refusing to speak to anyone. She would only nod or shake her head and she seemed to be suffering from sporadic shivering fits. The querent then posed the question, drew the chart and — deeply concerned by what she saw — asked me to look at it. Eventually I felt able to make a judgement.

This sister is a married woman of about thirty-nine years of age with several children. She was clearly unwell, and my task was to try and discover if her condition was serious. It is a third party question, and sisters come under the dominion of the third house, so for convenience I have also drawn the chart turned, to show the third house rising. We then have the body of the sister in the place of the Ascendant.

The first consideration is: Does the chart describe the symptoms? Venus, lady of the first, and therefore ruler of the body of the sister, is in the third house of communication and Gemini, the sign of communication, opposed by Neptune, whose influence causes confusion and worry. Shivering or shaking seems well described to me by an opposition of Venus and Neptune across the Gemini-Sagittarius axis. The ruler of the sixth house of health is Mercury, and he is retrograde in mute Cancer, a most telling indication of silence.

The next consideration is: Is she really sick? As with the last example we can first apply the general rules — if there is no aspect between the rulers of the first and sixth, there is no sickness, and if the Moon is Void of Course there is usually nothing to worry about. Venus, lady of the first, and Mercury, lord of the sixth, are in no aspect here. Jupiter is in good aspect with the cusp of the first, and the Moon is in good aspect with the lady of the first from the sixth. These are testimonies against sickness.

Arguments for sickness are: the Moon — *besieged and under duress in the sixth house,* and Venus applying by square to Saturn at the cusp of the sixth. Both of these conditions look ominous. The Moon besieged by Mars and Pluto looks particularly nasty. Indeed it was this condition which so worried the querent when she first drew the chart, because before the chart is turned it appears in the eighth house. However, Venus — significator of the subject, disposes of the Moon and her besiegers, so it does not suggest serious illness. Whatever the condition represents, the subject has the power to handle it herself. I must say that my first reaction was to wonder

at the state of her kidneys, for the sign of Libra has dominion over
the kidneys. Then there is the other condition — Venus applying
to a square of Saturn at the sixth cusp, with Saturn in the sixth sign
of Virgo for good measure. The subject is moving relentlessly towards
a confrontation with Saturn, and a rather unhealthy looking Saturn
at that. I gave this aspect a lot of thought, and decided that although
it probably represented a difficult period from a health point of view,
it did not signify serious illness. In coming to that conclusion I took
note of the fact that both Venus and Saturn were in common signs,
that Saturn was not generally badly aspected, that Venus is by nature
benefic, and that Saturn was ruler of the actual querent (the subject's
sister), and may well have been reflecting her worry and concern.
On balance I did not think she was seriously ill at all.

So what is wrong with her? As I have said, the besieged Moon
in Libra could suggest a kidney complaint, but because of the
disposition by Venus, this does not seem to be the key to the problem.
But look! Before the chart is turned to put the subject on the
Ascendant, the Sun is angular upon a critical cardinal degree, with
Mercury retrograding back from combustion. The chart is pointing
most forcibly to this Sun-Mercury conjunction. It must mean
something. Now when the chart is turned from its natural order
to put the subject upon the Ascendant, the Sun-Mercury conjunction
appears upon the fifth cusp. This cusp, together with the sign of
Cancer, immediately brings to mind child-bearing. Is it possible,
then, that the lady has lately become aware (Mercury) that her child-
bearing capacity (Cancer fifth house) has ended (combustion)? Could
she have begun the menopause, and is her distressed condition a
result of a psychological reaction to her changed state?

So I thought that the lady had reached the critical stage in her
life where she had begun to experience 'the change'; she was
distressed by the experience and had produced the strange physical
symptoms for that reason. She was not really sick, for although at
first sight the chart looked ominous, Venus (her significator) had
dignity in her own terms and disposed of the Moon and her besiegers;
Mercury, lord of the sixth, also had dignity in his own terms. I thought
that the resolution of the problem lay in the lady's own hands. She
must come to terms with her changed physical condition. It would
be difficult because the final aspect of the Moon is a square with
the Sun, but Mercury soon goes direct and makes good aspects with

Uranus and Saturn, and the final aspect of Mercury being a sextile with Saturn suggests her acceptance of the physical implications of her age. The combustion between Mercury and the Sun cannot take place again within the sign of Cancer, so the crisis has passed.

A week or so later I learned that the lady had indeed begun the menopause, and her condition was a response to that experience. I was also fascinated to learn that she had a longstanding kidney complaint for which she had been receiving treatment for some time. The lesson here is that we must always allow the original chart to be of assistance; it had been pointing strongly to the angular Sun, in a cardinal sign, upon a critical degree, and it was the Sun that turned out to be the key to the problem. Disposition is also important in this case. The Moon, Mars and Pluto were in Libra — the sign in which Venus has dignity. Venus therefore disposes of all three, giving the subject power over them.

Figure 70: How long will my mother-in-law live? Will she ever come out of hospital?
The querent's mother-in-law was in hospital after suffering a 'massive stroke', and he wanted to know whether she would ever come out and how long she was likely to live. Despite the appearance of the question, it was put with a good heart. The querent's main concern was for his wife, who was very worried and distressed.

Here is another third-party question. The chart is radical, so we must find the significators. Mars is for the querent but what about his mother-in-law? Sticking to my assertion that the tenth house is the house of a father, and the fourth that of a mother, I must look at the house fourth from the seventh (the fourth house of the querent's wife) to find the mother-in-law. She, I say, is ruled by the Sun, lord of the tenth house of the chart. I have again turned the chart, and the mother-in-law's house is now upon the Ascendant.

As soon as this is done, the condition of the mother-in-law is graphically described by the chart — the Sun conjunct Jupiter in Cancer in the twelfth house. She is in hospital (twelfth house), in intensive care, and I could not imagine a more telling representation of intensive care than Sun conjunct Jupiter in Cancer. The chart shows that she is exactly where she should be. So the chart confirms what we already know, and we must now decide whether the mother-in-law is likely to recover enough to come out of hospital and how long she is likely to live.

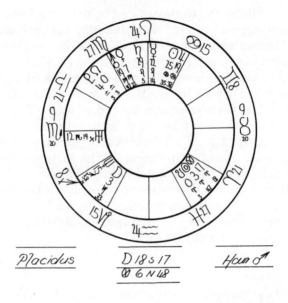

Figure 70(a).   How long will my mother-in-law live? Will she ever come
out of hospital? 18 July 1978 2PM3 GMT 51N46 0W28

Figure 70(b).   The above chart turned to show 10th house rising

I have frequently perused all the ancient rules and aphorisms concerning whether someone will recover and when; whether the illness will be long or short; whether illness is curable or incurable, and so forth. In the end I have found them of little assistance, and I tend to go back to the chart and use my common sense. In this case the ruler of the sixth house, Saturn, is in the fixed sign of Leo, conjunct the Ascendant with the Ascendant applying to him. Saturn is malefic, and in the fixed sign of Leo he is seen to be solidly malefic, and the indication is that the body of the mother-in-law (Ascendant) is very heavily afflicted. The ruler of the eighth is Jupiter. Although the Sun is separating from conjunction, the Moon will, in due course, bring them together again by opposition aspect. The Moon applies at once to a square of the Part of Death. All these factors do not suggest recovery, nor does the fact that the ruler of the eighth is stronger than the ruler of the subject. My judgement was that the lady would not recover. I thought that she would probably benefit from treatment, suggested by the Moon trining Venus in Virgo, but in my view the eventual opposition of Sun and Moon symbolized the end of her life, as did the Ascendant applying to a conjunction of the malevolent Saturn, lord of the sixth. The lady will not come out of hospital because she is stuck in the twelfth with no way out of that situation.

As to the likely time of her death, I reasoned as follows: the Ascendant lacked 4 degrees of a conjunction with Saturn; for an angular house and a fixed sign the Generally Accepted Measure of Time is 1 degree per month, thus four months. The Moon applies to an opposition of Jupiter by 16 degrees; for a succeedent house and a cardinal sign the Generally Accepted Measure of Time is 1 degree per week, thus sixteen weeks. The Moon applies to an opposition of the Sun by 22 degrees; again a succeedent house and a cardinal sign = 22 weeks. So I judged she would live between sixteen and twenty-two weeks more.

I do not have the exact date of death because the querent never mentioned the matter again after I gave him my judgement, but I heard from a mutual friend that the lady had died about four months later without coming out of hospital, and he told the friend that I had been 'quite accurate'.

Figure 71: Will Mary die?
This question was asked by a student of astrology about an elderly

friend of hers after she discovered that Mary was seriously ill in
hospital. It was one of those charts that was overtaken by events.
It was drawn up and considered, but no firm judgement was arrived
at, and a few days later Mary died. At the time it was drawn up
I looked at it, but I did not feel able to give a final judgement, so
I put it aside. Some time afterwards I was given the time of death
and decided that it was a suitable case for an astrological post-mortem.

The querent asked the question about a friend, so the friend is
shown by the eleventh house of the chart. She is therefore signified
by Mercury; and if there was any doubt about their relationship,
the chart itself clearly resolves it by putting the Moon in the eleventh
house. There is no doubt about the question: 'Will she die?' It is
an eighth house question, so the significator of Mary's death or
otherwise is Saturn, Mary's eighth being the sixth of the chart. To
avoid any confusion I have redrawn the chart to show the eleventh
house rising.

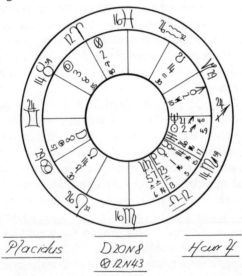

Figure 71. Will Mary die? 24 November 1980 10PM34 GMT London
Original chart turned to show 11th cusp rising

The main significators are Mercury and Saturn, but they are not
in relationship with each other. The Moon being in Mary's house

can be taken as her co-significator. She does have a relationship with Saturn, an interesting separating square. Had that aspect been applying instead of separating, it would have encouraged me to judge that Mary would die, but separating aspects indicate things that have occurred, not things that are about to happen. The Moon has three applying aspects — trine Mercury/square Pluto/trine Uranus. In view of the strength of the Moon in her own sign of Cancer, I did not consider Mary to be in great danger. However, Jupiter is ruler of the sixth house and he is closing to a conjunction of Saturn. This does suggest serious illness, and the separating Moon indicates that there has been a recent crisis. Nevertheless, at the time I was not prepared to say she would die.

Now with the benefit of hindsight, I must point out one vital fact that was not considered at the time the chart was first drawn. Mary's main significator is Mercury; the condition of Mercury then must reflect the condition of Mary. He sits right upon the sixth cusp in Scorpio (the eighth sign) applying to a conjunction of Uranus. This is further testimony that the lady is seriously ill, and because Mercury is in a fixed sign, it suggests that the illness cannot be easily cured; also, Uranus tends to show incurable illness. The Moon will shortly bring these two (Mercury and Uranus) together by first trining one and then the other. The fact that the Moon cast a benefic trine aspect does not mitigate the maleficity of the basic conjunction. Here is one indication of the outcome, but even more important is the close square of Mercury to the South Node in the eighth house.

Opinions vary about the effectiveness of the Nodes, but Ivy Goldstein-Jacobson holds that they are important in questions about sickness. She further states that: 'Any planet or angle in the same degree as the Nodes points to a catastrophe, casualty, fatality or tragedy in a horary or natal chart. The more far-reaching when a malefic is involved. If the horary planet is one degree applying the affliction is about due. If it is one degree separating the trouble has already occurred.' In this case, with Mercury almost exactly square the South Node in the eighth house, would I have been justified in judging that the sickness would result in imminent death? Maybe so, for that is what happened. Mary died four days after the question was asked.

Figure 72: Is there any hope of recovery?
This question was asked by letter. The querent had a friend, Pamela,

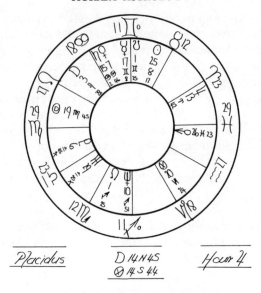

Placidus   ☽ 14 N 45   Hour ♃
                  ⊗ 14 S 44

Figure 72.   Is there any hope of recovery? 16 May 1975 6PM36 GMT
50N26 3W30

who was unfortunately suffering from cancer. She had been
undergoing treatment by radiotherapy, injections and faith healing.
The querent wanted to know if there was any hope of recovery. As
is usual in these cases, I set the chart for the time I read the question
and located it for the place the letter was written from.

Once again, the question is about the querent's friend, so I have
turned the chart to show the eleventh cusp rising. The significator
of Pamela is Mercury, and since this is a question about the possibility
of death, it is an eighth house matter, and Mars is ruler of Pamela's
eighth house. We must also consider Saturn, ruler of her sixth house
of health.

Mercury is strong in Gemini and applies to three other bodies;
square to the Part of Death, square to Mars (eighth ruler) and trine
to Uranus (joint sixth ruler). However, Mercury does not complete
his square with Mars or his trine with Uranus, because when he
reaches the 23rd degree of Gemini he turns retrograde. The only
applying aspect Mercury can immediately make is a square to the
Part of Death. The condition of Pamela must be reflected in the

condition of her ruler, Mercury. Although he is strong in the sign of mentality, which testifies to a great strength of mind, he is slowing down in motion and about to retrograde, which we may equate with the state of the subject's health. These first considerations do not promise recovery.

If we look to the Moon as a co-significator of the subject, we see that she is not in good condition either, she is besieged; she is between two evil forces — Saturn and the Part of Death. This besiegement may be mitigated to some extent by the Moon's applying good aspects to Jupiter and Neptune, but she is still besieged. Mars, ruler of the eighth house applies to an opposition of the first house (the house of life), and upon the perfection of that aspect, Mars will occupy the degree of the highly malevolent fixed star Scheat ('malevolence of sublime scope'). Furthermore the Sun occupies the degree of another malefic fixed star, Caput Algol, and the Sun is ruler of Pamela's twelfth house. There is little assistance from benefics in this chart. Venus is closing to conjunct Saturn, and Jupiter is moving to square Saturn.

It is true to say that the Moon has a way out of her besieged condition through a reception with the Sun; for the Moon occupies the sign of the Sun's dignity and the Sun occupies the sign of the Moon's exaltation. If we allow that reception, the Moon moves to 3 Taurus, right into the eighth house, and the Sun moves to 25 Leo, conjunct the 12th cusp. From her new position the Moon would apply well to Venus and Saturn, but from that eighth house position she must still square the Sun at the twelfth cusp. Not a pattern to inspire optimism.

I judged that there would be no recovery, since I could find nothing to promise it. However, I had access to the nativity, and with such serious questions I like to consider the birth-chart when it is available.

Figure 73 shows a most interesting natal pattern. It is the Virgo-Pisces polarity which stresses sickness and confinement. Saturn in Pisces opposes Neptune in Virgo and takes in Jupiter at the Ascendant, to form a mutable T-square; Neptune square Venus at the Ascendant; Mars is closely conjunct Saturn in Pisces; the Sun, ruler of the eighth, squares Uranus; Mercury, ruler of the sixth, is quincunx Neptune. It is Neptune that stands out, on his own upon the ninth cusp in the sign of health (it is notable that the cancer from which Pamela was suffering had its origin in the thigh, a part

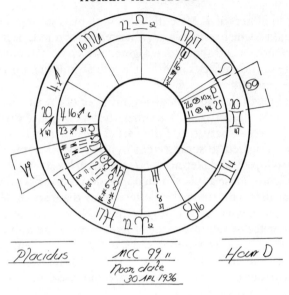

Chart turned to show 11th house rising
Figure 73.   Nativity of Pamela 23 January 1936 5AM33 GMT
50N26 3W30

of the body associated with the ninth house).

Secondary progressions for 1975 show the progressed Ascendant conjunct radical Sun and square progressed Uranus, thus heavily emphasizing the radical square; the progressed Midheaven also activates the radical Sun-Uranus square, and although the aspect is a sextile, it cannot overcome the power of the natal square. The progressed Sun conjuncts the progressed Saturn. Over the previous five years the progressed Sun had made a conjunction with radical Mars, radical Saturn, and finally progressed Saturn. This symbolizes considerable pressure on the life-force (the Sun), and by 1975 the body of the native must have been in a very weak condition.

It will be noticed that the Midheaven-Nadir axis of the horary chart falls square to the progressed Sun-Saturn conjunction, and that the Moon of the horary opposes the Sun of the nativity. After studying the nativity and the secondary progressions I could find no reason to alter my judgement that there was no hope of recovery.

Pamela died on 19 November 1975 at approximately 2.00 a.m.

	0 1 2 3 4 5 6 7 8 9 10 11 12 13 14 15 16 17 18 19 20 21 22 23 24 25 26 27 28 29 30

Natal Positions
23 Jan 1936
5AM33

```
☉             ♂ ♄        ☊           ♃ ☽        A M ♀       ♇
2             6 8        11          16 17       20 22 23    26
♎             ♓ ♓        ♏           ♐ ♏        ♐ ♎ ♐       ♋
3             46 5       44          6 57        47 52 31    10 ℞
♅                                    Ψ ☿
1                                    16 17
☋                                    ♏ ♎
37                                   27℞ 35℞
```

Secondary Progressions for 19 Nov 1975

```
♅             ♂         ☉ ♄ ☽ Ψ ☿             ♃          ♇
2             7         12 12 14 15 16          22         25
☋             ♈         ♓ ♓ ♋ ♏ ♎             ♐          ♋
40            34        18 46 15 29℞ 8          12         25℞
♏                       ♀
3                       12
♐                       ♎
7                       7
A
3
♎
0
```

Transits for 19 Nov 1975

```
♂ ♄ ♅                   ♀ Ψ ♇          ♃           ☿ ☊           ☉ ☽
1 2 4                   9 10 10        15          20 21          26 27
♋ ♌ ♏                   ♎ ♐ ♎          ♈           ♏ ♏          ♏ ♀
30℞ 56℞ 17              59 58 48       33℞         28 31          7 49
```

Horary Positions for 16 May 1975 6PM36

```
☽             ♇ ♀       Ψ           ♃ ♄         ☿            ☉ ♂        ♅
3             6 7       10          13 15        17           25 26      29
♌             ♎ ♋       ♐           ♈ ♋         ♓            ♉ ♓        ♎
28            45 46℞     51          42 2         8            17 23      25℞
```

Figure 74. Secondary progressions re Figure 73

GMT, just over six months after the date of the horary question. She died on a Full Moon which fell within 2 degrees of the horary Sun.

Figure 74 sets out the details of the planetary positions of all the charts involved in this case in a readily recognizable form. Figure 75 isolates the main pattern and shows the striking correlations with the horary chart.

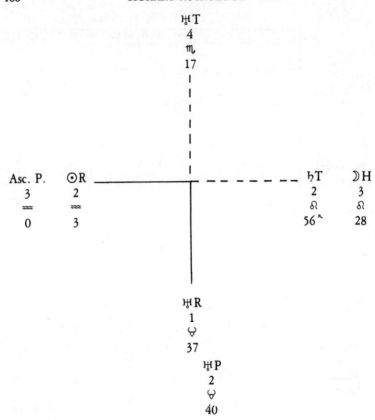

R = Radical positions
P = Progressed positions
T = Transit positions
H = Horary positions

Figure 75.   Potent pattern re Figure 74

17.
MISCELLANEOUS

In the preceding chapters I have concentrated on questions which mainly concern the personal affairs of the querent, or someone in whom the querent is interested. Sometimes, however, people are moved to ask questions about other matters. My last four examples fall into this class.

Figure 76: When will the recession lift in the United Kingdom? This question emerged in a conversation I was having with a friend about the serious economic situation facing the nation. How do we begin to approach such a chart? My own approach is to view the chart as that of a nation, and relate the house and planets of the horary chart to the affairs of the country. According to Charles Carter (*An Introduction to Political Astrology*), the dominion of the houses and planets in a national chart are as follows:

First house: The nation as a whole, a unitary political body.

Second house: The economy of the country and its material prosperity; all that is related thereto, and those engaged therewith.

Third house: Education, schools, and literature of all kinds, especially periodical publications. Post Office, radio, telegraphs. All modes of transit. Neighbouring countries.

Fourth house: Land, houses and the produce of the land. Possibly crops (but some authorities give crops to Virgo and the sixth house). The common people.

Fifth house: All forms of national pleasure and enjoyment, amusements, entertainments, theatres, sports and all forms of speculation. Children and the birth-rate. Public morality and scandals. Society and high social functions. By tradition it is also the house of ambassadors.

Sixth house: Public health, the armed forces and the civil service. The working population and the Labour Party.

Seventh house: Relations with foreign countries. It is said to be the house of open warfare and enmity as well as of treaties and alliances, but friendly nations must also be considered under the eleventh house, and all foreign relations have some connection with the ninth house.

Eighth house: Death and public mortality. Death duties, taxation, insurance. Financial relations with foreign countries. The Privy Council.

Ninth house: Long-distance travel and communications. Law and religion.

Tenth house: Rulers, whether monarchs or presidents, the government in a general sense, the national prestige. This is regarded as the most important house in mundane astrology and planets here have a wide significance.

Eleventh house: Parliament, friends of the nation, local government. In my own opinion this house also controls fraternal associations such as trade unions.

Twelfth house: All philanthropic and reformatory institutions, prisons, hospitals, asylums, etc., secret and occult societies. Underground movements and enemies of the state. Monasteries and other forms of institutional religion.

The Sun: Represents the supreme authority of the state, royalty and nobility, those in supreme control over whatever department of national life is under consideration.

The Moon: Relates to the mass of the people, and to land and crops. It is the significatrix of women.

Mercury: Literature, the Press, education and all means of communication. It is said to have an effect upon general trade.

Venus: Rules the social and festive side of national life, society and art. It is the planet of peace, but in time of war it is the planet of victory.

Mars: The armed forces and all trades that serve them; engineering; violent crime. Often significant in connection with epidemics.

Jupiter: Church and clergy, law and lawyers; banking and insurance. It is the planet of prosperity and peace.

Saturn: Landed and house property; the formal side of the state; the law as a restraining influence.

Uranus: The administrative officers of state and their functions; the administration of power. Physical power, particularly electricity.

Neptune: Hospitals and charitable institutions. The navy and merchant marine. Treachery, scandal, muddle; the underworld and crime. Brewing, drink trades, oil and chemicals. Theatre, films, music and art.

Pluto: Mines. All practices that bring the hidden to light. Crime and war.

These rulerships are given for guidance. Opinions may vary considerably about the dominion of the various houses and planets, and much investigation and correlation needs to be done in this sphere.

The question — 'When will the recession lift in the United Kingdom?' — is principally concerned with two factors: (1) the economic health of the country, and (2) unemployment.

The ruler of the second house of the chart is Venus, and Venus is shown weak in Virgo. Virgo is the sixth sign and is therefore concerned with the mass of the people, or the working population. The Moon (people) is in square aspect with Venus, and since Venus is angular, it is strongly emphasized in the chart and describes the conditions that provoked the question.

The Sun, as we have seen, is said to rule those in supreme control of whatever department of national life is under consideration, and in this case it must be the government. The government (Sun) is about to conjunct Pluto, and therefore the nation is bound for a Plutonian experience. If we allow the Sun 1½ degrees of orb on either side of the exact conjunction, and we take a degree for a year, it will be about two-and-a-half years before the Sun clears the Pluto influence. The astrologer might then consider that the recession would begin to lift around the middle of 1983.

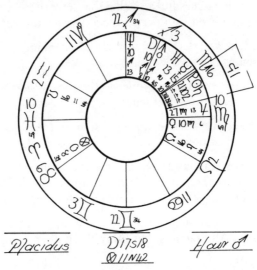

Figure 76.
When will the recession lift in the United Kingdom?
13 October 1980 4PM0 GMT 51N46 0W28

Another promise of better days is the fact that Venus will eventually make a conjunction with Jupiter. Both are in the sign of Virgo, so that conjunction would suggest a great improvement in the employment situation. However, the conjunction does not actually occur in Virgo. It is not until they reach the first degree of Libra that they meet, and when they do so they fall in close connection with the restrictive Saturn, and he is strong in the sign of his exaltation. From this pattern I would deduce that although the recession might 'bottom out' within a year, and then gradually begin to lift as the Sun moves away from the influence of Pluto, the effect upon unemployment will not be as beneficial as the people might hope. In support of this theory, note the position of the Moon in optimistic Sagittarius: she is in square to Venus but looks ahead to bring Venus together with Jupiter, but she fails to bring it about within Virgo.

Between 1980 and 1983, British industry was obliged to transform itself and the consequent 'shake-outs' had the effect of vastly increasing unemployment, and now at the beginning of 1984 we stand facing the new year with a problem so vast that it cannot be speedily resolved. It is interesting that Neptune sits at the Midheaven of this chart, and Neptune equates with oil. The Sun and Pluto are in good aspect with it, and so the influence of this vital commodity has done much to ease the drastic transformation the nation has been obliged to undergo.

Figure 77: *Will the invaders be repelled?*
As soon as I heard of the invasion of the Falkland Islands by Argentina I posed the question above. I also set a chart for the actual invasion, taking the moment of dawn as the potent moment. Shortly afterwards I presented these charts in a lecture to the Astrological Lodge of London and reasoned as follows.

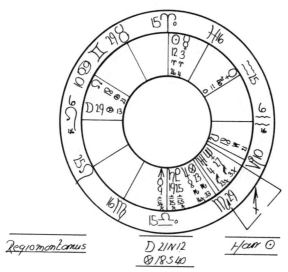

Figure 77.
Will the invaders be repelled?
2 April 1982 12PM15 GMT 51N46 0W28

The first house represents our nation, the seventh house Argentina as an open enemy. The fourth house the territory belonging to the nation, the Falkland Islands. From the position of Saturn in the fourth, the presence of Argentina upon our territory can be plainly seen. The Sun in Aries well represents Britain (ruled by Aries), and is moving to oppose Saturn. The promise is of confrontation and thus war. If the Sun and Saturn are to come into conflict with each other, then the Sun will prevail, because although both are exalted, the Sun approaches the Midheaven of the chart and is elevated, while Saturn is retrograde. I therefore thought that the Argentinian presence would be removed from the Falkland Islands, and that the timing might well coincide with the great conjunction of Saturn and Pluto. Despite the strong indications of conflict shown in the chart, I thought there was a possibility that it could be avoided because Saturn and Venus were in reception. Venus is ruler of the eleventh house (friends of the nation), and by her own nature she suggests negotiation. So I thought that the matter could be resolved through negotiation, and Venus in Aquarius well symbolized America.

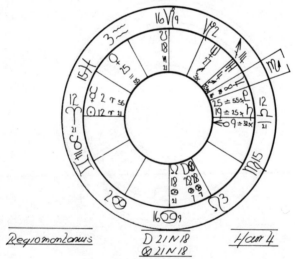

Figure 78.
Falkland Islands invasion by Argentina
2 April 1982 10AM22 GMT 51S42 58W0

The interesting thing about this chart is that while Saturn and Venus are in reception, the Sun remains opposed to Saturn and in no aspect with Venus, so although a settlement by negotiation might have been possible with Argentina, Britain seemed unlikely to accept any compromise. The leader of our country must be shown by the tenth house, and its ruler is Mars — which is upon the degree of the malefic fixed star Vindemiatrix is the Star of Widowhood. By one means or another, the removal of Argentina from the Falklands seemed to me certain.

Looking at the chart I had drawn for the invasion (Figure 78), it occurred to me that the timing of the operation was certainly not selected by an astrologer. The ruler of the Ascendant weak in Libra and retrograde and upon the Star of Widowhood, the Moon Void of Course and the South Node at the Midheaven: hardly a pattern indicative of success. The influence of America in the eleventh house of this chart can be clearly seen again.

The whole Falklands Campaign is worthy of a study to itself, but such a study does not fall within the scope of this book.

Figure 79: Will England suffer a Channel tunnel?
It is illogical I suppose to think that the Channel is an effective defence against aggression in this day and age. The value of a natural moat has been superseded by nuclear missiles and sophisticated aircraft, but it was only forty years ago (within my lifetime) when the channel, bad weather, mist and fog played a vital part in saving these islands from a German invasion. There is something special about being an island, and I for one have no desire to see access to these shores made any easier than it is already. All my instincts are against a Channel tunnel, and I suspect that millions of my countrymen share this view. I should regret such a link with as much feeling as I witnessed our transfer to the metric system, and I would prefer to see rabies safely confined to the domain of our Continental cousins. It was in this eccentric spirit that I posed the above question.

For something that goes under the earth we should look to the fourth house. It is interesting to find Neptune there in Sagittarius — a tunnel beneath the sea giving access to foreign lands. The Moon in Aries (the people of England) applies to Neptune by trine aspect, and that seems to symbolize easy communication with the Continent. Yet the ability of the Moon to perfect her aspect with Neptune suffers massive frustration from the Mars-Saturn conjunction in the second house. Clearly the project is denied because of the expense. The Sun (the government) applies to a good aspect of Jupiter, ruler of the fourth. Now this could be seen as the government being in favour of a tunnel, and there is no impediment to their perfection. On the other hand the aspect can also be interpreted as the government (the Sun) being secretly (Pisces) in sympathy (trine in Water) with the instincts of the people (fourth ruler in Scorpio). My judgement is that there will be no Channel tunnel because in their hearts nobody really wants it, but the cost of the operation can always be put forward as an excuse for doing nothing about it; and so we will remain protected by our natural moat 'against infection and the hand of war'.

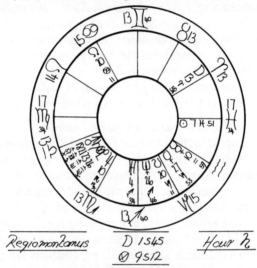

Figure 79.
Will England suffer a Channel tunnel?
26 February 1982 6AM48 GMT 51B46 0W28

Figure 80: Was Richard III responsible for the death of the princes?
Allow me to leave you with a challenge, a historical mystery. This question was put to me by a young lady one night in a pub, when she was engaged in a spirited defence of the character of Richard III. She regarded the common belief that he was responsible for the death of his two nephews as vile slander, and was much concerned that his reputation should be rehabilitated. Upon such matters do the English rage passionate in the comfort of their favourite inns.

Richard Duke of Gloucester served his elder brother King Edward IV with faithfulness and valour. Upon the death of his brother on 9 April 1483, Richard was named Protector in the royal will. This did not suit the Queen, who, while Richard was away in the north of the country, caused a resolution to be passed through the Council replacing Richard's protectorship with a regency council, and sent for her son the young Edward V to come from Ludlow to London for coronation. Richard intercepted the young Edward on the road and sent him to the Tower of London. The Queen took sanctuary with her younger son Richard at Westminster. The Duke of Gloucester with support from many nobles and his own men from Yorkshire decided to bid for the throne. He removed the young Prince Richard from sanctuary and sent him to join his brother in the Tower. It was then alleged that the marriage of King Edward IV to his queen, Elizabeth Woodville, was superseded by an earlier marriage contract with one Eleanor Butler, and that the two princes were therefore bastards. This left Richard Duke of Gloucester as the only true heir to the throne. At the end of June 1483 Parliament met and produced a petition inviting Richard to take the throne.

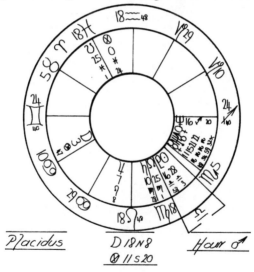

Figure 80.
Was Richard III responsible for the death of the princes?
21 October 1978 7PM27 GMT 51N46 0W28

After some reluctance he graciously accepted and was crowned on 6 July 1483. The princes were not seen after the autumn of 1483, and although there is no conclusive evidence that Richard had them murdered, it has been commonly supposed that he did. Richard was born at Fotheringay Castle, Northamptonshire, on 2 October 1452. He died leading a cavalry charge on 22 August 1485, and was the last English king to die on the field of battle. With him died the House of York, and so began the Tudor dynasty.

There you are — was Richard guilty, Yea or Nay?

CONCLUSION

It is only within the last decade or so that horary astrology has gained serious recognition in modern times. Apart from the writings of Lilly and the work of some Hindu astrologers, there are very few books on the subject, and most of these draw heavily on Lilly. As I have mentioned elsewhere, the book I found most valuable when I began to study horary astrology is *Simplified Horary Astrology,* by Ivy Goldstein-Jacobson.

It was an article by Joan Rodgers in *Prediction* many years ago which first drew my attention to horary astrology, and I was immediately captivated by the idea, and it was Goldstein-Jacobson's book that gave me the grounding I required in the art. Lilly recorded what was known at the time in which he lived, and he drew from the ancients, but his own rich and colourful experience has been passed down to us over 300 years. Goldstein-Jacobson took the essence of the ancient rules and enlarged upon them with her own experience. I hope this book follows in that tradition, because it represents my own experience honestly and frankly presented.

Although I have continually stressed the importance of the basic rules — considerations before judgement, the traditional modes of perfection and the conditions which deny perfection — I must say that I do not agree with some of the traditional restrictions. I can find no consistent evidence to justify an old view of the *via combusta,* and I cannot agree that a significator falling between the degrees 15 Libra to 15 Scorpio is ineffective. Nor am I convinced that a New Moon in horary astrology is as malefic an indication as tradition would have us believe. I need much more proof of this, and valuable work is being done on this matter by Maurice McCann. I am not so sure that a seventh house Saturn is invariably an indication that the judgement of the astrologer is at fault. Despite my personal reservations it is always wise to be cautious.

On the other hand I have found that a retrograde seventh house ruler frequently prevents the astrologer from delivering judgement for some reason. I must say that I have found, time and again, that a good, uninterrupted applying aspect between Sun and Moon is a very powerful indication of success, and the only time I have known it fail is when one of the Lights has been upon the degree of a malefic fixed star. I have ample evidence to justify the traditional maleficity ascribed to the fixed stars Caput Algol and the Pleiades, and the evil influence of Serpentis at 19 Scorpio survives without a shadow of doubt. All this I pass on to you for information, but as I have said *ad nauseam,* you must be guided by your own experience.

Anyone who reads Lilly's *Christian Astrology* or *An Introduction to Astrology* will see that very many instructions were given for the resolution of various classes of question. I have refrained from repeating these, and I have also refrained from giving copious lists of matters, persons and things which come under the dominion of the various houses and planets. My reasons for such omissions are these:

1. modern life is vastly different to life in the seventeenth century, and we must adapt planetary symbolism to modern requirements;

2. aside from the basic rules, the various guidelines set out by Lilly and other astrologers for the judgement of various types of question are merely the experience of that astrologer. It is a grave mistake to take the view that if Lilly or someone else did not mention or sanction something it is not valid. The experience of other astrologers cannot be given the sanctity of firm rules. Every new moment of time is unique and is reflected in the heavens by a unique planetary pattern. That pattern must be interpreted anew by the individual astrologer and related to the matter under consideration. My main purpose in this book has been to demonstrate by example how to approach a chart and how to apply oneself to the resolution of a question.

3. It is wise to understand the difficulties the heavens have in producing answers to all manner of questions. We have to accept what we are given and make the best of it. If all the planets are contained within the space of two houses, and neither of those houses relate to the matter under consideration, but the chart is a valid one, do not reject the chart as unreasonable; the answer is there somewhere, and you must use all your ingenuity, intuition and any other powers you possess. Your approach should always be flexible.

Accept if you will the basic rules of horary astrology; they are an essential application to any chart. From then on you are on your own. Repair to your study or garret, and in its quietness commune with the chart. It will have a message to give, and that message will be intimate to the circumstances of querent and quesited. It might take a long time and much mind-bending to decode it, but it is there somewhere. It is a matter between you and the heavens. There is no foolproof formula that will provide an automatic resolution.

Good luck with your divinations.

BIBLIOGRAPHY

An Introduction to Political Astrology, Charles E. O. Carter. (L. N. Fowler.).

The Lives of the Kings and Queens of England, Antonia Fraser (Book Club Associates, London).

Simplified Horary Astrology, Ivy Goldstein-Jacobson (Privately published in USA).

Christian Astrology, William Lilly (not generally available).

An Introduction to Astrology, William Lilly (Newcastle Publishing Co., Hollywood, California).

Improved Perpetual Planetary Hour Book, George Llewellyn (Llewellyn Publications, St. Paul, Minn. USA)

The Fixed Stars and Constellations in Astrology, Vivian E. Robson (Aquarian Press).

INDEX